How to Raise a

COMPETITIVE FIGURE SKATER

A Book for Parents

DORIS E. BODMER

Mehler Press
Downers Grove, Illinois

Mehler Press, 239 55th Place, Downer's Grove, IL 60516

ISBN: 0-9711949-0-4

Manufactured in the United States

Cover and interior design by Sans Serif, Inc., Saline, Michigan

Cover picture—a group of happy local students in training at Ice Castles International Training Center in Lake Arrowhead, California. Photo by Cindy Lang.

CONTENTS

FOREWORD

This book is informative, educational and highly recommended for all parents and others involved in the "raising" of competitive figure skaters. Doris Bodmer has drawn on her considerable experience and insight acquired over the years as a competitive skater, coach and then judge to offer a book that will provide guidance through the intricacies of a wonderful sport. I congratulate Doris Bodmer on the thought and effort that went into the preparation of this book and the thorough and clear manner in which she has covered the subject.

CAROL HEISS JENKINS

PREFACE

Raising a competitive figure skater is difficult. Most parents don't know what they are getting into—especially how much time and money they will spend. Their goals are fuzzy; some see the big O of the Olympics as the goal for their children, others just want lessons so their child will skate without dragging one foot behind. Most skaters will achieve a goal somewhere between these two extremes. The book hopes to help parents understand this very special, complicated, and fascinating sport—what options there are and how best to take advantage of them.

I have tried to give you an idea of the cost, but please be careful; prices vary and are only **very approximate**. They can be different, depending on the location in which your child skates.

I am using an imaginary little girl called Vicky to represent a typical skater. Her parents as well as her coaches, friends, and foes are not actual people but typical of the skating world. Vicky could just as well be Victor. But because there are more girls than boys who take up the sport, I decided on Vicky. Boys have a better chance to place well in beginning competitions simply because there are fewer of them. In top competitions it is equally difficult for both sexes.

ACKNOWLEDGMENTS

My first thanks go to my husband without whose help and encouragement this book would never have been written.

I also would like to extend my sincere thanks to Carol Heiss Jenkins for writing the Foreword. Carol is a member of the World Figure Skating Hall of Fame, National, World, and Olympic Champion, and now a world-class coach in Cleveland, Ohio. Many other coaches also gave me invaluable help. Cindy Perpich, with many encouraging and helpful suggestions; Libby Scanlan, always with witty and amusing advice; Debbie Stoery, for her encouraging remarks and her great knowledge about the sport which she was willing to share with me.

Judges were most helpful as well. Jan Serafine, with valuable suggestions; Gay Barnes, who is a whiz in organizing material; Rosemarie Santee's great experience; and Joe Serafine, longtime president of the United States Figure Skating Association (USFSA), U.S. Hall of Fame member, and a very insightful and knowledgeable judge. Furthermore, Ed Mann, the USFSA accountant who read the chapter on "How to Read a Result Sheet" with so much care and patience, and the USFSA, for permitting me to quote from the *Rulebook*.

Further I wish to thank the USFSA for permission

to reproduce various statements of the *Rulebook*, as well as photographs and Harry N. Abrams, Inc., for letting me publish the poem by George Meagher. Many thanks also go to Cindy Lang for letting me use the cover photo and others.

The Four Branches of Figure Skating

There are four main forms of figure skating: Singles, Pairs, Dance, and Synchronized skating. I will discuss all of them throughout this book.

Singles

I will stress Single skating more, because most skaters begin as single skaters.

Pairs and Dance

Any time is O.K. to start Pairs and Dance. Make sure the boy is bodily developed enough to lift his partner. The longer the partnership lasts, the better it is for the unison of the couple, which is a very important component of Pairs and Dance. To switch partners often can hurt unison, and is therefore not advisable. But what are you going to do if your couple fights like dog and cat? Or the girl grows a head taller than the boy? Those are problems specific to Pairs and Dance. Also remember not to neglect single skating even if you are a pair team. Difficult side by side jumps are demanded in higher competitions, which can become a big problem if the single skating has been neglected. There are the same competitions held for Pairs and Dance as for Singles. Most often these three disciplines compete at the same date.

Synchronized Skating

The great difference between Synchronized skating and any other form of figure skating is that this is really a team effort. The competitions are not held at the same date as Singles, Pairs, and Dance, simply because of the great numbers. Synchronized Competitions involve team spirit as an important aspect. There are a minimum of 12 and a maximum of 20 skaters in each synchronized team. Of course there are also difficulties (like tripping over each other, and who is to blame for making the entire line fall over). More and more skaters thoroughly enjoy the camaraderie and the different challenges synchronized skating offers. Many skaters do both, and if it did not go so well for them in Singles, they can look for-

ward to the next Synchronized competition. As a parent I would certainly encourage the skater to join a synchronized team. Should other forms of competition become more and more demanding, the skater can always drop the synchronized team at that point.

Is There a Difference in Regard to Figure Skating for Boys and Girls?

Yes, I think there is. The main part has to do with body changes in puberty. Girls often change in body structure. Their hips become somewhat wider and they have a tendency to gain weight. Therefore, the now-demanded triple jumps become much harder to do. No women have landed triple Axels in their programs since Midori Ito about 10 years ago and Tonia Harding, who could do them but then lost this skill. Triple Axels are very difficult jumps for girls, however most men competing in Worlds can do them. Boys seem to improve in general for a longer period of time than girls. As their shoulders and arms get stronger with age their jumps improve. At 25, men can be very competitive. For women, careers in top-level competition often do not last that long. Of course there are exceptions. Don't get discouraged as you begin to read this book, and think your daughter will be through at 15. First of all, we have recently seen world-champion women at the age of 27 and secondly, many avenues are open to skaters to make this sport a pleasure for life.

The Start of It All

Introducing Vicky
(Our Fictional Skater)

It is a rainy Sunday afternoon and Vicky is bored. She is an active five-year-old jumping on the furniture, hopping on the bed, and irritating her little brother, Rob. Her mother Anne has a bright idea. "Lets go ice skating," she says—and that is the start of it all.

Anne and Vicky drive to a rink in the neighborhood, rent skates, and try to wobble around the slippery ice surface. Anne's ankles hurt, her knees ache and she soon gets off the ice, collapsing into one of the seats on the bleachers. She watches Vicky—sliding, slipping, falling, wiping off her snowy gloves. Relentlessly, Vicky tries, and tries again, and soon actually stands up quite straight. Her cheeks are red with the cold and the excitement. "Let's go now," says Anne. "No," Vicky replies simply.

"Would you like a hot chocolate?"

"Oh no, later," says Vicky, as she nearly crashes into the boards.(She can't stop on skates yet.) Even though Anne really wants to get home, she is proud of her little Vicky, of her perseverance and pluck.

Parents, always try to remember your beginning skating experiences with your children. First of all how proud you were, and secondly that you really let them skate because they so enjoy it. Don't let ambition spoil the joy, don't let disappointments sour your children's love of the sport.

When Anne describes her Sunday afternoon to her husband Paul, he suggests taking Vicky for lessons. How little he knew how much time, money, and energy would be spent at the rink after making this suggestion.

Registering for Group Lessons

Four or five years is a good age to start skating lessons. Younger than that is all right if the child likes it, but some are really too young and the experience becomes more tearful than pleasant. What a child learns in a whole year, starting at age three, can easily be accomplished in four months at the age of four or five.

When Anne and Vicky go to sign up for lessons, they learn that classes are taught through the Ice Skating Institute (ISI). The Greek alphabet—Pre-Alpha, Alpha, Beta, Gamma, Delta, names the beginning classes, followed by

Free Style classes which range from FS (Free Style) 1 to FS 10.

Vicky is registered for eight weeks once a week in the Pre-Alpha class. Anne learns the fee is $80, and includes free practice time. This is reasonable; to Anne it sounds quite expensive, but she has not had much experience yet with what skating costs. Skate rental is $1 per lesson. Anne thinks skate rental will be cumulatively expensive, and asks if she can buy skates at a department store. That is not a good idea; such skates are usually made with little support and blades which, due to their cheap steel, glide badly on the ice. Often Pro shops in the rinks themselves have knowledgeable personnel who know what to advise. The rink where Anne and Vicky chose to skate happens to be a rather figure-skating-oriented rink and the head of the Pro shop is very versed in fitting boots. Usually rental skates at a rink are better than the skates of a department store. Anne opts for new skates for Vicky. Renting skates for the first class and only buying if you really think the child likes it is also a good option.

Buying the First Pair of Skates

Skate fitting is very important and going to a knowledgeable person is well worthwhile. Vicky and Anne wait for Pete, who was recommended to them. After being told that Vicky will be going into Pre-Alpha, Pete measures

Vicky's foot carefully. She does not need a very stiff pair of boots, nor does she need expensive leather or luxurious blades. But Anne's money-saving idea, that Vicky should get boots nice and big so she can grow and still wear them for a long time, unfortunately does not work. A skate must fit snugly, otherwise the heel of the foot slips up and down in the boot, and Vicky will get blisters. Pete knows what to advise. A reasonably stiff pair of boots with adequate blades for around $250 will serve Vicky well. The price will go up as Vicky climbs the skating ladder. (For a more advanced skater the price can vary between $600 and $700 depending on the skater's need.) Sometimes secondhand skates are available for a much more reasonable price. Care must be taken that these skates really fit, as otherwise they can cause foot problems and a lot of frustrations.

Make your skaters wear the new skates at home (with guards on, so as not to scratch the floor). Wear them at least two to three hours on different days before going on the ice with them. That really helps to prevent blisters and foot pains, so often caused by new boots.

Skate Guards and Protective Gear

Skate guards are necessary. The plastic ones are for walking with. There are also cloth guards which skaters put on their blades when the skates are packed in the bag. The "walk-in " skate guards need to come off when the skates are packed in the skate bag. The blades need to be wiped dry with a soft cloth. Blades left wet make the soles of the boot soggy and screws will loosen. A skater needs to learn early to take care of the equipment, which is an expensive and very important tool. Walking on the floor with unprotected skates is bad. Even if the floors are rubber or plastic there will still be dirt on them which can harm the sharpness of the blades. The worst is concrete, which tends to be full of sand and grit. Don't let your skater run through the parking lot without guards.

Knee pads are helpful because kids often fall hard on their knees in new boots and blades, especially on figure skates due to the toe picks. We dress figure skaters like little elves and expect them to fall like well-padded football players on a surface which is harder than a football field. Thick woolen hats are also a good idea as they can protect a child when falling on the head. For tot classes, many instructors advise helmets. When skaters get more advanced protective gear changes, but I do feel that not protecting your hip, for example, when it is already black-and-blue from falling on it, is just silly.

THREE

What Do Skating Associations Offer?

The ISI

The Ice Skating Institute (ISI) was founded in 1959 in the United States by Michael Kirby and other supporters. Michael skated with Sonja Henie in her later shows. He wanted to make skating more affordable for everyone, and started what was then the Ice Skating Institute of America in 1960 in Chicago. Up to that time, a skater who wanted to compete had to belong to a club affiliated with the United States Figure Skating Association Club fees were often high, which discouraged many from taking part in the sport. The story goes that a line of prospective skaters, all around a Chicago Rink, formed when ISI classes were first offered. The price was very affordable, and many people wanted to take advantage of it. The key concept with ISI then, as now, is **recreational.** ISI is not bound by International Skating Union rules, therefore ISI is free to be very creative in their competitions. There are very many innovative ideas to be found in the *"Ice Skating Institute Competitors Handbook."* Often the rink your child is skating at will have a handbook available, but you can also order one by calling the Ice Skating Institute in Dallas, Texas, 972-735-8800. You or your child have to be an ISI member in order to do so. The cost of membership is $7.

ISI introduced freestyle competitions where nobody gets lower than sixth place, by only listing the first five skaters on the result sheets. Even if the group consists of 12 skaters, anybody not mentioned on the sheet automatically places sixth. A big difference from the USFSA is that all ISI competitions are team competitions. All skaters competing (apart from being placed 1-5) earn team points for the rink they represent. The more events a skater enters the more team points will be earned, as the emphasis is on participation. There are no elimination rounds. The ISI gives joy to many a skater by providing a competition outlet in a variety of categories. There is a niche for every skater to participate in.

ISI Tests

Although private lessons are also an option for ISI skaters, group lessons are encouraged. Michael Kirby was a great advocate for group lessons and wanted to give skaters a chance to compete even if they could not afford many, or even any, private lessons. After each ISI group lesson course there is a test to see if the student is ready to pass onto the next level. The judges for these tests are normally the class instructors and the tests are held during class time in an informal way.

ISI Free Style and Other Competitions

For young skaters who start in the ISI program it is usual to do their first competitions for this association. Competitions range from the simple Pre-Alpha competition to the difficult FS-10. In areas where ISI is popular, many competitions are held and it is easy for skaters to find places to compete nearby. The ISI competitions are based on test level. For example, if the skaters have passed FS-1, they also have to compete at that level. Parents, this is a point to consider. Don't absolutely insist that your children test out of their level, because if they should want to compete, they just may not be competitive at the higher level. Let the instructor make the decision when to test. It's okay to repeat a class. Competition fees are about $45 for the first event and $10 for each additional event—interpretive skating, synchronized skating, spotlight, and more. For details consult the *ISI Handbook*. Entry fees may vary but they are around this amount.

The ISI freestyles are set and determined by various maneuvers the skater has to perform. Doing the wrong maneuver can cost the skater valuable points. A relaxed attitude is very much encouraged. However, I have seen parents get very uptight at ISI meets, taking them too seriously. That is a mistake, but then most parents at ISI competitions are not very experienced in handling competition pressure, and a fall of their five-year-old can upset them all out of proportion. Remember, parents, there are going to be literally hundreds of competitions for your children if they stay in the sport. Try and tell yourself that it really does not matter that Johnny fell down. If he cries, offer a Kleenex. If you get angry, check yourself. First of all, Johnny did not want to fall down and secondly, it really does not matter. On the contrary, Johnny will have learned that to fall down and not do so well is okay (what is important is to get up as soon as possible). In the next competition he will have learned from that fall and will do better.

Who Can Be a Judge in ISI?

The judges are most often skating instructors who have been certified by ISI. (This is very different from USFSA, as discussed later on).

Sometimes parents and skaters feel the results were not fair. This feeling is very common in figure skating. You can't measure it like a running competition with a stopwatch, or a long jump competition with a tape measure. One judge is very impressed with the height of the jumps even if the landing is not perfect. The other judge just looks at the landings, deducting for the wobbles, and does not take the height into account. In big international competitions one sees the judge of the skater's country holding up higher marks for them. Maybe this happens because the judge knows his skater better and is not likely to miss anything, or the judge really understands the music because he heard it so often—who knows? What I have learned in becoming a USFSA judge myself is that judges really try to be fair. Yes, mistakes can and do occur, but parents, please believe me when I say that judges try their very best and don't dislike a certain skater. They may not approve of a skater's style, but they will not mark any skater down because they don't like him, his club, or anything personal. If it is a small ISI meet or World competition there always will be somebody who does not like the result. My advice is to live with it. If you really think you can't live with inconsistencies in judging you may be better off having your child take up a more measurable sport. A consolation is that if you stay in skating long enough you will feel it's unfair once, but another time you will feel as if your skater has been given a gift. In the end it will even out. Don't let a seemingly unfair placement spoil the fun of skating. Explain to your children that this is a subjective sport. Don't harp on unfairness. Underline the fun of competition and the love of the sport. Give your skaters advice on how they can improve—then they can do something about it—work to a goal. Just to say "it was unfair" really helps nobody and makes the skater feel powerless and at the whim of some uncontrollable and unfortunate destiny. Of course if the skater is outstandingly good judging will be much easier. But then it's impossible to have all skaters be outstandingly good.

Who Should Switch from ISI to USFSA and Why?

In areas where ISI is taught, the first classes a child participates in are ISI classes. It is natural that also the first competitions will be through ISI. A skater can participate in the ice shows, join an ISI synchronized team, compete in some interpretive skating, etc. Why should anyone want to join USFSA? Because for the really dedicated skater USFSA is more challenging. Some children really want to skate every hour of every day. They see that the best skaters compete for USFSA and they want to try the same. If you can spend the extra time needed and can financially afford it, I definitely would say "Go for it." I think the time to switch from ISI to USFSA should be made around the FS-4 level. (At the time your skater is learning the Axel.) But this is a very individual decision. If the financial aspects are too difficult, if the child is not that interested in skating, or if skating is really difficult for the child to do, I would say it is better to stay with ISI and have fun than to stress yourself too much going into USFSA. Sometimes skaters make compromises and take tests in USFSA as well as ISI but compete in ISI as it is less taxing. Age plays a role in skating. If you want to switch to USFSA at age 16 and compete after having skated only ISI since the age of five you will have a rough, if not impossible time. If you switch at the age of eight or nine it will be much easier to meet the greater demands of USFSA competitions. It is always a good idea to consult some coaches to help you make this decision. A coach can judge better if skaters have enough ability and if it is a good idea for them to go with USFSA. Don't be shy about asking other coaches, maybe coaches of other rinks, to take a look at your skater. This way you can get an unbiased opinion. Some skaters opt to do both for a while—ISI competitions as well as USFSA competition.

USFSA

"The United States Figure Skating Association is the national governing body for the sport of figure skating in the United States and is so recognized by the International Skating Union (I.S.U.) and the United States Olympic Committee (USOC)" (from the USFSA Rule Book 2001, page xix).

The USFSA was formed in 1921 with seven clubs as charter members. Now they have 535 member clubs.

USFSA Tests and Competitions and Their Learn-to-Skate Program

If a skater has ambitions for National competition, ultimately leading to Worlds and Olympics, or if skaters want to participate in the USFSA test structure, they must join a USFSA club or become an individual member of the USFSA. In general, to join a club is preferable because clubs try to help their skaters. Of course only few out of many thousands of skaters make it to Nationals or Worlds. Olympics mostly stay a dream—a dream not to be squashed by parents. Let the child dream by all means. However, you as parents remember that it is very rare that a skater gets to the Olympics. It is for the fun, the learning, and the discipline that your children participate in the sport. If you understand that idea correctly at the start, it will help you no end all through the career of your skater.

Like the ISI, the USFSA also offers a learn-to-skate program, to join you can, but do not have to be a member of the USFSA. It is called the Basic Skills program. Rinks either offer the ISI or the Basic Skills learn-to-skate programs, depending on the geographical area.

The similarity of the programs involves the *learn-to-skate programs only*. As the skaters get more advanced, the ISI emphasizes skating as recreation, whereas the USFSA is competitively oriented.

USFSA Tests

As does ISI, USFSA also offers tests to qualify for competitions. These tests are much more formal than their ISI counterpart. Skaters have to uphold the high standard the USFSA demands. On special days, USFSA judges are asked to come to a rink to judge certain tests. Coaches are not allowed to judge. Students sign up for whichever level they are ready, and are judged on a nationwide standard. There are three judges for each tester (not counting the trial judges who may be present) and failures occur quite frequently. Parents, it's quite all right if your child fails once in a while. It is not shameful; your children are not bad skaters or have got bad coaches—they just did not meet the standard the judges wanted to see. After four weeks the test can be retried, and the judges can be asked by coaches and skaters what to improve. Failing in school may be bad, but failing a skating test can be a positive learning experience, not a misery.

Most skaters have private instruction to prepare for USFSA tests. It is not like ISI, where you can take group lessons only and expect to pass the test leading up to the next level. To pass high USFSA tests helps skaters in their careers; for example, if they want to join a Synchronized team, if they want to teach, take part in an ice show, or judge.

There are eight moves tests, eight freestyle tests, nine dance tests, and five synchronized team tests. Synchronized team tests are not mandatory to join a synchronized team.

The following levels for singles are:

Moves Tests	Free Style Tests
Pre-Preliminary Moves	Pre-Preliminary Free Skating Test
Preliminary Moves	Preliminary Free Skating Test
Pre-Juvenile Moves	Pre-Juvenile Free Skating Test
Juvenile Moves	Juvenile Free Skating Test
Intermediate Moves	Intermediate Free Skating Test
Novice Moves	Novice Free Skating Test
Junior Moves	Junior Free Skating Test
Senior Moves	Senior Free Skating Test

USFSA Competitions

Beginning Competitions

As mentioned earlier, the USFSA also offers a learn-to-skate program (basic skills) and there are small competitions held in this program, which resemble the ISI beginning competitions.

Nonqualifying USFSA Competitions

As soon as the skaters get more advanced there are many "nonqualifying" USFSA competitions. These are designed to prepare the skater for the more advanced qualifying events. Qualifying events mean that one competition leads to a more advanced one if the skaters qualify; i.e., if they come in the first four, for example.

Nonqualifying competitions end with the last day of that competition.

I have not gone into all the details and rules. For more specific information it is good to purchase the *Rulebook* printed by the USFSA.

It can be ordered by calling the USFSA at 719-635-5200 in Colorado Springs. Even though the *Rulebook* seems overwhelming and often confusing at first sight with all the paragraphs and clauses, as your skater progresses the *Rulebook* will become clearer and is a big help. Make sure that you always have the current *Rulebook* for the year. Rules tend to change.

All skaters must belong to USFSA to participate. The choice of which competition to enter is normally made together with the coach. Especially at the beginning level it is best to choose a competition where the coach will attend—even if coaches do charge expenses and time. Young coachless skaters remind me of lost puppies, mothers or fathers often feel rather at a loose end standing at the rink door with their child, and not quite knowing what to say.

Sometimes nonqualifying competitions offer final rounds, sometimes they don't. Sometimes groups are selected by age level, sometimes they are not. These decisions are made by the local organizing committees. Apart from freestyle, competitions can offer compulsory events, footwork events, spin events, and dance. What level skaters can compete at depends on their test level. For example, if the skaters have taken their Juvenile test they will compete at the juvenile level. Therefore, to be too ambitious and want to take as many tests as possible can have a drawback. Many skaters hold back on their tests because they will be more competitive at a lower level. When children are ready to go on to a higher level they will want to do so, to show the judges and peers what they can do, but as parents don't force your skaters in a level they are not competitive at. Discuss this with your coach.

It helps skaters to watch a nearby competition before entering one. In contrast to ISI, skaters can perform more freely in the allotted time what they can do best. Some rules, however, do exist and should be strictly adhered to in order to avoid deductions. Again, consult the *Rulebook* to make sure.

From the Intermediate level on, when USFSA skaters in qualifying competitions have to perform two programs, the "short program" as well as the longer "freestyle program," there are specific requirements for the short program. The freestyle program also has some restrictions but there are fewer.

USFSA Qualifying competitions

The first qualifying competition for skaters is the one in their region held once a year. I have included a diagram on the following page to show how a skater can go up the ladder from Regionals all the way to Worlds with the crowning achievement for seniors (very few seniors indeed) the Olympics every four years. At qualifying competitions rules are set by the USFSA. What age level, how many skaters make final round, etc., is all predetermined and can be looked up in the *Rulebook*. For some skaters it's a great goal to qualify and compete at Regionals; for others, Regionals is only the first step of many.

FIGURE 1.

GOING UP THE LADDER TO THE OLYMPICS

Regional championships

New England	Eastern Great Lakes	Central Pacific
North Atlantic	Southwesterns	Northwest Pacific
South Atlantic	Upper Great Lakes	Southwest Pacific

Sectional Championships

Eastern	Midwesterns	Pacific Coast

National championships

World championships

Olympics every four years

Other Competitions the USFSA Offers

Collegiate Competitions

Sanctioned by the USFSA, these competitions have become much more popular and cater especially to skaters who are in college. They are not as demanding as the regular USFSA qualifying competitions, but give skaters a great opportunity to compete. They go up to National level. You will find more details in the *Rulebook*.

State Games

State games include many sports. Figure skating is sanctioned by the USFSA and ISI. State games are also becoming more popular. They include, among other sports: Skiing, Snowboarding, Ice Hockey, and Figure Skating. It is a less stressful atmosphere than at a qualifying competition, and lots of fun for all. The first three skaters in each group are eligible to compete at the State games of America.

Special Olympics

This competition is for skaters with some disabilities and is instituted to have a therapeutic effect as well as to be fun for these skaters.

Various International Competitions

Worlds
For International Competitions a committee of the USFSA decides who would be a good candidate.

For Worlds, the National champions in each discipline will be definitely going and then one or more skaters, depending on what the results were the previous year. Again, details will be in the *Rulebook*.

Other International Competitions

There are quite a few international competitions; some are for Novices, some for Juniors, and the best known ones are for Senior skaters. The Grand Prix, ending in a final where each winner can receive up to $120,000, is one of the best known and is also shown on television. The Four Continent competition is another championship on a very high level. I believe it was originally instituted to be a competition similar to Europeans'. American, Asian, Australian, and African skaters had no competition like the European skaters, so the Four Continent competition was introduced.

What is Meant by Amateur (Now Called Eligible) Skaters versus Professionals?

A warning for parents: If you hear that the winner of the Grand Prix can get $120,000, don't imagine dollar bills will be floating to your skater. File such thoughts under "Dreams." To make millions in skating does happen, but it happens only to the famous few. Enjoy your child's skating and learning, but don't think he or she will become a millionaire. Very few do.

It used to be strictly forbidden to earn any money to be considered an eligible skater, and only eligible skaters were allowed at Worlds, Olympic, and National championships. This has changed; USFSA competitors may now accept money for commercials, for teaching after having reached the age of 18, and for ice shows as well as for some competitions, which is demonstrated by the Grand Prix mentioned before. In these cases a skater sponsorship contract must be obtained from USFSA headquarters. You also must send notification to your club sanction officer, local sanction officer, and your sectional vice chairman.

For National champions to be allowed to earn money for shows and commercials is a big change. Some of these very special champions make a lot of money these days. The division between "Professionals" and "eligible skaters" has become fuzzy and is often hard to explain clearly. But to make big money, as said before, only applies to the exceptional few. Keep in mind that it is parents who usually pay for the majority of all skating expenses.

Who Judges USFSA and International Competitions?

Rigorous training is needed to become a USFSA judge. Trial judging is the start. Experienced and advanced skaters can be accepted in the accelerated program; for others, trial judging can take a long time. Maybe years. A judge slowly works his or her way up the ladder from low test to a higher and higher level. To attend judges' schools is mandatory. For qualifying competitions, judges again have to trial judge before being able to judge "when it really counts." All judges, referees, and trial judges are volunteers. They are not paid, except for their expenses. So you can be assured that judges really love skating; otherwise they just would not do it. From my experience so far, it can be thrilling and most gratifying to judge. I have yet to have one experience where I thought that a judge was knowingly unfair or favoring a skater. Mistakes can and do occur but it is not because of a lack of commitment by the judges.

PSA (Professional Skaters Association)

Although this association is for coaches, parents can take advantage of many things the PSA offers. One of the main functions of PSA is to train coaches. Coaches get "rated" by PSA. As parents you can get an idea if the coach has had serious training by looking at their ratings. This is not to say that unrated coaches cannot be just as good or even better for your skater. But rating gives parents a guideline. A master rated coach will usually ask higher fees for private lessons than an unrated coach. If unrated coaches should ask excessively high fees compared to the rated coaches, ask them why.

The PSA also offers instructional videotapes. Especially for moves tests these can be very helpful to your skater, and you can compare and see if your skater looks anything like the skater on the tape.

The PSA is very helpful in educating coaches in ethical behavior. They have yearly meetings and young coaches can listen to very interesting lectures of world coaches and get education in many facets of skating. "The USFSA recognizes the PSA as the official coaches' education, certification, and training program." (USFSA *Rulebook*, Year 2001, page xix).

FOUR

Going Back in History

Long before the USFSA, the ISI, and the PSA were formed; long before indoor skating rinks were built; and long before skating was so very popular with children, there was skating for enjoyment. In Holland, where there are many rivers which freeze during the winter, people put bones underneath their shoes, drilled holes through them, and tied them on with strings. They started to glide up and down the rivers many hundreds of years ago.

There is even a Saint of Skating. She is Saint Lydwina. It seems she became a saint due to a rather sad reason. She fell down skating, so the story goes, and became very ill after that. She bore that illness with such bravery that she was sanctified. The terrible fall Lydwina took happened as long ago as 1396.

The Accident to Saint Lidwina (1396)

FIGURE 2. Here is a picture of Saint Lydwina having taken her terrible fall in 1396 (World Figure Skating Hall of Fame Museum).

Is Figure Skating a Sport or an Art?

The answer is that it is both. This is also one of its great fascinations.

You have to perform the difficult jumps, the spins, the steps, and strong and sure speed is vital because otherwise however great the artistry is, it does not help in the final scoring. You have to have the difficulty. The trouble is, you have to execute this difficulty very artistically. That is why the second mark, the presentation mark, is the determining factor in the long program if there is a tie. When Lebedeff edged out his figure, skating was a sport, but today when Michelle Kwan skates like a wonderful flowing feather on the ice it is much more than just a sport.

Let's take a jump to 1830 when the first skating club was formed in England. Club members were mainly men and these men started to skate most intricate circles which, later on, developed into what was called "figures."

Compulsory Figures

As skating increased in popularity, competitions started to be held. Etching out ever more intricate patterns on the ice and repeating the tracings was the goal.

It was not jumps and spins and artistry or musicality which made you a champion as late as 1908—it was drawing the most intricate patterns on the ice with your skate. It would be most difficult for a skater of today to draw the following patterns.

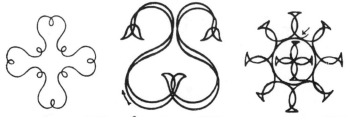

b. ALEX. LEBEDEFF 1883   f. N. PANIN 1897   g. A. CUMMING 1908

FIGURE 3. Special Figures invented by the skaters themselves were the determining factor of who won the competitions. Here are three figures skated by Mr. Lebedorf, Mr. Panin, and Mr. Cummings. For skaters of today it would be nearly impossible to repeat these intricate patterns. (These figures were performed between 1883 and 1908) (World Figure Skating Hall of Fame Museum).

Out of these patterns later evolved what the older generation remembers as compulsory figures. The patterns or figures were no longer invented by the skaters, but completely prescribed. **Figure skating** is still named after figures. If a skater wanted to be recognized in figure skating they had to practice eight's and three's in circles, as well as brackets and loops. Pictures of these standardized figures can be found at the back of the USFSA *Rulebook* today (2001 edition).

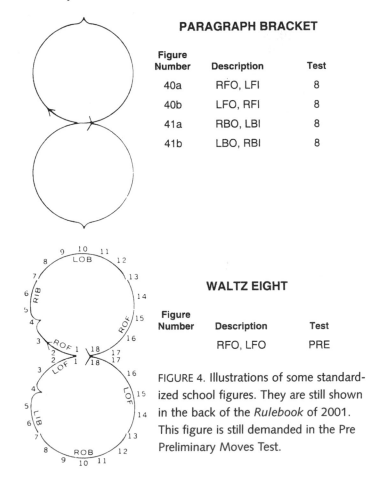

PARAGRAPH BRACKET

Figure Number	Description	Test
40a	RFO, LFI	8
40b	LFO, RFI	8
41a	RBO, LBI	8
41b	LBO, RBI	8

WALTZ EIGHT

Figure Number	Description	Test
	RFO, LFO	PRE

FIGURE 4. Illustrations of some standardized school figures. They are still shown in the back of the *Rulebook* of 2001. This figure is still demanded in the Pre Preliminary Moves Test.

FIGURE 5. Dick Button, the famous skating TV announcer as a young man (without the beard) etching out a figure at the World Championship in Milan. Note the controlled body position, following the tracing on the ice with tremendous concentration. Dick also is a member of the World Figure Skating Hall of Fame.

Tests still can be taken in figures today, but skaters doing them are becoming rarer and will probably soon disappear. Figures are no longer necessary to qualify for competitions. A great deal of time and money went into figures. Many hours of concentration were necessary to really master a good figure. Until the 1970s only the eight best skaters in figures at a USFSA competition were allowed to skate their freestyle.

Apart from being very expensive for the skaters, they are boring to watch if you are not a connoisseur. TV shows did not get an audience if they showed figures.

The Olympic Committee eliminated figures in Olympic competition in 1988. Soon other countries began to follow suit, not demanding figures anymore in their competitions, and the USFSA joined them with some regret.

Freestyle, the now dominant form of skating, was so named because after etching out good figures, skaters then had to show some moves, jumps, and spins in a "free manner," without restrictions. Good "figure skaters" often did not do well in free skating and vice versa. Figures were very heavily weighted in the scoring. When I started to skate, figures counted 70% of the total mark, with free skating adding only 30%. This percentage went down as time went on. Before eliminating figures altogether, they only counted 30% toward the final score. Older skaters and older coaches who used to teach or compete in figures will discuss ad infinitum how much figures helped or did not help free skating. Some claim figures helped a great deal; others deny that they were helpful at all.

A Tribute to a Famous Coach

Of course there have been, and still are, many famous coaches of figure skating, but there is one very special one and that is Guss (Gustav) Lussi. He was born in Switzerland and then moved to the United States and actually taught 16 world champions. That is quite an achievement. Dick Button (the TV announcer and World and Olympic champion) took lessons from Guss for over 10 years. Guss called his method of teaching "systematic figure skating" and understood the importance of crossing your legs in a double jump (before his systematic approach to figure skating the legs were often taught to be side by side and often swung wide in a double jump, which would make triple jumps impossible). Guss invented the flying sit and flying camel spin, and much more. He opened the first indoor summer skating rink in Lake Placid as early as 1932.

FIGURE 6. A picture of Guss Lussi and Dick Button at Lake Placid (Figure Skating Hall of Fame Museum).

The Start of Moves Test

What to do instead of compulsory figures became the question. Christy Krall, now Senior Director of the Athletic Program of the USFSA, carefully thought out a series of steps called "Moves in the Field" (Moves, for short). There are no jumps or spins to be performed, but edges with difficult turns, power, and flow. The turns consists of threes, rockers, counters, and brackets which were done in figures, and mohawks and choctows, which are done in dance. Moves in the field combines all these turns with fast, powerful, and flowing edges. The continued practice of powerful skating is definitely helpful to free skating. Moves need to be very well executed to fulfill the function Christy and others have so well thought out. It is a very good idea to purchase the PSA tape on "Moves in the Field." There are two tapes showing how the moves should be done. The tape can be ordered by calling the PSA office directly at 507-281-5122 in Rochester Minnesota.

Every move from the most basic to the senior move is explained very well by the well-known coaches Janette Champion and Becky Calvin. Good skaters perform the moves and you, as a parent, can get an idea what is expected of the skater. You can furthermore study the patterns of the moves and understand what your child is aiming at. You can learn with your skater what the primary focus of each move is, what the particular moves are called, and what the patterns look like. I do not think that is interfering with the coach. Don't teach, just watch together, and remember that judges also watch this tape and use it as a standard. Another good idea is to video-tape your child doing the moves test when they are ready to test, and look at the tape together—even better, all three of you: the coach, the skater, and the parent. Then right after your skater has completed the move, change tapes and look at the same move done by the skater on the PSA tape. That should give you a good idea as to what is required and where your skater needs improve-ment, and what looks a little "funny" and should be changed. Again, parents! Don't teach. Just look at the videotape. If you have questions, ask the coach. If the coach wants to charge some lesson time to watch with you, that may be well worthwhile, possibly more fruitful than practicing the same mistakes without much im-provement day after day on the ice. The *Rulebook* is also very helpful in showing the patterns and mentioning the primary and secondary focus of each move.

FIVE

Instruction Begins for Vicky

Now that we have discussed the different associations and some of the history of figure skating let's go back to Vicky, who is ready to take her first skating class.

Vicky's First Alpha Class

Vicky, proud with her new skates, knee pads, gloves, and a hat arrives at the rink for her first skating lesson. The rink, normally showing a white shiny ice surface, is so full of skaters Vicky can't even see the ice. It seems the whole town decided to go skating today. Instructors with clipboards are busy writing and at the same time screaming out class levels. Anne ties Vicky's skates the way Pete showed her, fairly tight up to the ankle, tightest around the ankle, loose on the top so her feet don't cramp. She does this about four times, because Vicky complains, "they're too tight," Anne loosens the laces; "Now they're too loose," "Not so tight on the top," etc., etc. Anne vows as soon as possible, Vicky will have to learn to tie her own skates. That's right, she should become less and less dependent as time goes on. Skate tying is the first step. In rink lobbies you often see a 10-year-old holding up her foot, while eating popcorn and waiting for her "servant" (her mother in this case) to tie her skates. However much the child complains that she cannot get her skates tight enough, let her do it herself. She will soon learn.

Vicky looks a little overwhelmed with all the kids, the noise, and the general commotion. "Come on," encourages Anne and takes her daughter by the hand to the rink. It is a very important role for parents to be encouraging. The teaching should be left to the instructor, but if a child needs encouragement nobody can do it better than a parent who knows their child so very well.

"Your class is way in the far corner," points Anne. Vicky bravely skates out that way, falling twice over her toe picks; the knee pads help. The class starts. It quickly becomes evident that Vicky stands straighter on her skates and can bend her knees better than many others in her class. With immense pride in her little girl, Anne hears the instructor say, "good, Vicky" more than once. This is the first taste Anne is getting of how much she will enjoy Vicky's talent for skating. That's great but as parents, don't forget that however much pride and joy you get out of the sport, it is the child's thing. A parent is immensely important to a skater as an "encourager," as a mentor, as a "comforter," but a parent is not the skater. Don't get so involved in your skater's progress that you feel as if you had done a good thing when your child does well, and you had failed if your child does badly.

What about Other Siblings?

A few weeks later it is clear that Vicky is the best in her class and is promoted from Pre-Alpha to Alpha. Vicky begs for extra practice days, creating the first dilemma for Anne. What should she do with her little son Rob, who does not like to spend his time at the rink after school. Yet Anne can't leave him alone at home. At first she gives him quarters for the candy machine (bad for him—junk food) or pinball machines (expensive and dumb). That keeps him happy for a while, but it soon becomes evident that Rob is bored. He grumbles, and even says, "you always go where she wants to go."

With skaters, siblings often create a difficult situation. The figure skater in the family needs to be given more time. More money too.

A solution, but an expensive one, is if parents can get all their children to skate. There are instances where this has happened with success. To mention just a few. Michelle Kwan, world champion, has an older sister, Karen, who also skated and made it to National competition. Carol Heiss (World, Olympic, and four time U.S. Senior Ladies Champion) had a sister and a brother who also skated. Her husband, Hayes Jenkins, won Worlds and so did his brother David after him. Carol is now in the Hall of Fame in Colorado and a world-class coach, having coached many champions herself. Peter and Caitlin Carruthers won the silver medal in the Olympics and were four times the U.S. national champions as a pair team. (The interesting thing about Caitlin and Peter was that they were not actual siblings but both children were adopted by the Carruther family.) My godchildren, twins, made it to the Olympics for Switzerland as a pair team. The amazing thing with these two skaters was that their mother (a former competitive skater) was holding the two beautiful but weak-looking little babies when I came to visit in the hospital. She said, half jocularly and half seriously to me: "You know what—twins, a boy and a girl—I think I'll make them pair skaters. Maybe they'll go to the Olympics." It is very rare indeed that such predictions actually come to pass. My book emphasizes again and again that it is not the idea that your child skates because the Olympics is the goal, but that the skater skates for the love, the challenge, the learning, and the fun of it. Still, there are exemptions to every rule.

FIGURE 7. My godchildren Karen and Christian Kuenzle, first as little newborns, and then in their Olympic year in 1976.

FIGURE 8. Michelle Kwan, right, so far four-time world champion and a most admirable skater both in her wonderful ability to skate and in her great outlook on sport and life. She has a sister, Karen Kwan, who also made it to National competition. This picture shows Michelle and Karen (Photo by Cindy Lang).

FIGURE 9. Can you imagine what the mother of Hayes and David Jenkins experienced going through two world skating careers with her sons? They both won Worlds in different years. I have never seen a better flying Sit Spin than Hayes's (shown here). Both Hayes and David are World Figure Skating Hall of Fame members.

FIGURE 10. Illustration #10 showing both brothers Hayes and David Jenkins skating

The trouble with Vicky's brother Rob is that he does not like to skate. At least not figure skate.

Anne has a friend who happens to have a little boy Rob's age and she agrees to look after Rob on "skating days." That is a good solution for now. However, more problems will arise with Rob, and every time an answer must be found. It's fair that more money is spent on Vicky, as she really shows interest, but it's not fair to make Rob feel less wanted. Many skaters are an only child, or children with much older siblings. Then, of course, this problem does not exist.

FIGURE 11. Carol Heiss Jenkins as she competed with me at the 1952 World Championship in Davos.

FIGURE 12. Carol with her sister and brother, who all skated competitively. Mrs. Heiss had quite a job raising three competitive skaters.

Private Lessons

Vicky has now advanced to FS-1 and one day Vicky's teacher Becky walks up to the bleachers to talk to Anne. It is very unusual for her to talk to any mother, let alone leave the ice to do so. Becky sits down next to Anne.

"There will be a small ISI competition soon. Vicky is ready to enter. A few private lessons will help, of course," says Becky. Anne inquires innocently, "Whom do I ask for private lessons?"

"Oh, I can do it; I just had a cancellation."

If you have a promising young skater, remember that many coaches will make an effort to teach him or her in private lessons. It is not unusual to choose the class instructor, but maybe you are thinking of another coach. Possibly you have seen some coaches teach and were impressed with their interactions with their students. Becky well knows Anne is inexperienced. She takes advantage of Anne's lack of knowledge to get a good student. You can't blame Becky. She needs to make a living, but as a mother, don't go blindly with the first coach who offers her services. *You* are the customer and you can choose.

"How much are private lessons?" asks Anne.

"I charge $18 for 20 minutes," informs Becky.

"Ah, yes well, hmm," stutters Anne, "I'll have to think about it. . . . "

"It's only that I am very booked, and with the competition coming up . . . the after-school hours . . . you know." (Anne has yet to learn about the early morning hours.) Becky does not finish the sentence but makes her point very clear. Anne feels Now or Never. Becky notices Anne's interest.

"Shall we say Thursday at 3:30 then?"

Anne hears herself saying "That's great," and wonders at the same time about the extra money it will all cost, and where to find time for yet an extra afternoon of skating.

Vicky is only in FS-1 and really likes her class teacher, Becky. Becky's expertise is just fine for Vicky at the moment. Later, however, the question of teachers becomes much more complicated.

Becky goes back on the ice, and Anne wonders if it was right to agree so quickly to private lessons. What will Paul say? Will he be mad? As parents, it is good to be truthful with each other, even if it means an argument. To veil the truth, tell white lies, or worse yet, real lies, only keeps a very momentary peace.

I have seen mothers skimp on groceries to pay for lessons, or even go as far as to deprive the other children of braces for their teeth, all in order not to admit how much money went into skating. As much as you love skating and as much as you will do for the sport, don't sacrifice truth and family.

Talks Among the Parents

Anne tells Paul about the private lessons she arranged for Vicky. She tries to explain, but Paul does not quite comprehend. Vicky's skating is to him the same as Rob's baseball, like piano lessons were for Vicky. Parents expose children to activities like that if they can afford it. But isn't private lessons in skating going a little too far? In order to make Paul see the situation more clearly, he needs to get more involved with what Vicky is doing. He needs to watch a private lesson. See for himself that she really has ability. He should take Vicky alone to the rink once in a while, so that she feels her father's interest in something which is so important to her, and which she loves so much.

Preparing
for Competition

Although I am describing Vicky's FS-1 competition, much of what is said goes for all competitions, more advanced ISI ones, as well as USFSA qualifying and nonqualifying competitions.

Entry Forms and Music Tapes

After two weeks of private lessons, Anne gets the entry form for the competition from Becky. The entry fee is $45 for the free style event and $10 for compulsory moves (an extra event Vicky will enter). *Always make sure the entry forms are sent in on time.* Deadlines are rarely extended. (Also remember that for USFSA competitions a $90 entry fee for the first event is not out of line.)

Becky also informs Anne that she cut music tapes for Vicky. She chose the song *Tico Tico* and charged $50 for three cassette tapes and the cutting. Not a bad price. Once Vicky gets to advanced competition, often a "music cutter" will cut the tapes, and the price will be much higher. The whole question of music becomes much more involved as the skater progresses. For Vicky's FS-1 it is fine that the music was chosen by the instructor without any input from skater or parent. When the skaters become more experienced (even from the Pre-Preliminary or FS-4 level on), skaters should have a say in their music choice. They need at least two practice tapes, and one competition tape. All three must be clearly marked. For ISI: name, home rink, level, sex, age, and duration are required. For USFSA, name, level, club, and duration are necessary. "Play other side" is not enough. Two tapes should always be brought to competition. Both tapes must be ready to play; i.e., rewound. The "full" tape should be on **Side A. Side B should be blank** *to avoid possible confusion.* Look for the clear color leader which indicates that the tape has been rewound. A long delay may occur if the tape has to be rewound during competition, while the child, becoming nervous, stands on the ice getting stiff in the starting position. It is also important to punch the little bit of plastic out of the top corner of the tape, so the tape cannot be erased accidentally. Many skaters have lost some of their music because the recording button was accidentally pushed. With the punched-out little plastic square that cannot happen. Don't take a chance. You can always put a piece of tape over the little punched-out square, should you want to record over the tape. The spare cassette should always be handed to the coach. It is the instructor who will run with the spare tape to the music desk if something is wrong. Keep tapes in their cases so keys or pens can't get entangled with them.

Music

Music that is good to skate to may not be the music a child and especially a teenager will particularly like. Often a teenager will love very "boomy," "bangy," loud rhythms. That's fine for concerts or in the basement (the living room may be too trying for parents). But skaters are not performing for a modern concert; instead they perform a dance-related sport, for an audience (the judges) who may have rather standard tastes. An advanced skater will be able to handle more original music. Music with melody, with slow and fast parts which can be choreographed easily is a good choice. I don't mean music should not be original, but originality should not overshadow lyricism and melody. The trouble is that good music to skate to is used a lot. However, with careful research one can often find a fitting piece which is not overpopular. Also, the cutting has to be musically and technically correct. Pieces of music must fit together; cuts that are messy disturb the performance. Too many cuts can make the music sound disjointed; suddenly getting very soft and then very loud again can be distracting. Remember, the music is played in an ice rink, often a metal building with very so-so sound quality. It is a good idea to listen to suggestions from the coach, and for the advanced skater, from the choreographer. You, as a parent, can certainly have suggestions, but maybe they will not be followed if the skater and coach make a different choice. Don't harp on your choice. You are not the skater and unless you think the music chosen is really dreadful, try to think positively about it. Encourage the skaters to listen and come up with their ideas. For young skaters, who really have no idea what they like; asking them which music of other skaters they like can help with ideas. The choice of music should be a joint decision. When one party of the skating team (meaning parents, coaches, and skater) really dislikes the music it can cause difficulties. Coaches and skaters will hear that music nearly every skating day, and every day they say to themselves, if they don't like the music, "Here goes that music again . . . " Some skaters seem to know exactly what they want and it is often hard to persuade them that what they chose is not suitable. Others shrug their shoulders to any suggestions mumbling the irritating phrase, "I don't care."

The library is a good source for suggestions. One can take CDs or tapes home and listen to a lot of music.

Don't buy a stock of music you will not use. It will clutter the living room and irritate you because it was such a waste of money. If you hear something on the car radio you like, jot down the title (and keep that little bit of paper).

After all these suggestions it is true that any music can be very good and effective if it is interpreted well. Skaters, remember; a judge may be hearing this music for the first time, interpret it so well that it can be understood, and you will get high marks for presentation and originality. Another thing to remember is when you have a good music cutter, take his advice into account. If he really shudders at a cut, don't have him do it. Come to a compromise. As a general rule please, parents and skaters, understand music is a very important part of your performance. Give it thought, and have good quality tapes. It is very distracting for judges to hear the scratching and screeching of a tape, and worst of all, to hardly hear it at all. Also there are timing limits. If the music is too short or too long there is a mandatory deduction. Isn't it silly to have points deducted just because the tape was not timed right? But it happens so often that it is well worthwhile mentioning it here. As a general rule I would say that more often than not there is not adequate care taken in choosing and preparing such an important part of the performance—the quality and suitability and timing of the music.

Choreographers

Music leads into choreography. A young skater like Vicky obviously does not need a choreographer yet. For the young skater a good ballet teacher is more important. I would say a good guideline is to ask for help from a choreographer once the child has mastered the Axel and double Salchow. Before that, the instructor should be able to put together the program.

Many coaches will recommend certain choreographers they work with. Sometimes parents see choreographers work at the rink and like what they do with programs. Parents be careful, you may like the way a particular skater skates and it's not the choreography but the talent of the skater you like. Other times parents may opt to go out of town to a choreographer with their advanced skaters. For out of town choreography the video becomes a vital tool. Let the choreographer talk into the mike so you can hear what he has to say and review the tape when things get mushy and forgotten. Just as with the music choice, who choreographs the skater's program should be a joint decision between skater and coach, with the agreement of the parent. If skaters or coaches don't like the choreographer chosen it can cause problems. Skaters won't do the movements and expressions correctly, and if the coaches don't like the choreographer, they just "take out" everything in the program the parent paid a lot of money to have put in. The final say on the program should always be the coaches. Some musical coaches with a lot of ideas do the programs for the skaters themselves, which can be another very good option.

Competition Outfits

Back to Vicky. "Vicky should get a competition dress. Red would be nice with her *Tico Tico* music," suggests Becky. Outfits should show the skater's body off well and look attractive and tidy. (They don't have to cost a fortune.)

Sometimes parents of beginning skaters overdress their children. Instead of a simple dress there may be tutu-like undergarments making the skater look like a lampshade, or the sleeves are very wide and pronounced which draws too much attention to the arms. Arms in beginning skaters are often not yet used to perfection and should not be underlined with the outfit. It is important to show the outfit your child will wear to your coach. Not at the last minute, but in plenty of time, so that alterations can be made. It is also a good idea to have your child skate in what will be worn in competition before performance day. Sleeves may pull, sequins may scratch, and that can be disturbing and must be altered. Outfits should get more elaborate with ability level. A senior lady at Nationals wears a fancier dress than an Alpha skater. For girls; tights are to be worn *without underpants*. At first the child may object a little, but they get used to it. It looks bad if the underpants show. At the moment, beige tights which go over the boots called "mondos" are often worn. They are thick and the "underpants" question is not a problem. Furthermore the laces cannot hang out because they are inside the tights. For Synchronized teams such tights are a must. For other competitors they may be a good idea if they fit with the outfit. For young boys, well-fitting stretch pants and a nice shirt always look good. Mothers are often very clever sewing little girls' dresses, but can have trouble making well-fitting stretch pants for boys. Often a seamstress is a better choice. If stirrups are used to hold the pants in place with Velcro (which is pulled from one side of the pants to the other under the boot), make sure the stirrups really hold in place. If the Velcro strip comes loose it can cause falls, and disturb the skater's program.

A red dress is bought for Vicky, ready-made, for $85. Anne will sew a line of sequins around the neck. In it, Vicky looks just right.

In USFSA, judges must take outfits somewhat into account. A well-dressed skater is very pleasing to watch. The USFSA *Rulebook* has comments on dress codes:

> *The clothing of the competitor in all disciplines of figure skating must be modest, dignified, not garish or theatrical in design and appropriate for athletic competition. Clothing may, however, reflect the character of the music chosen. Clothing not meeting the foregoing requirements must be penalized by the judges by a deduction of 0.1 in the second mark (presentation mark).*

Clothing for Men cannot be theatrical in nature. Men must wear full-length trousers. Tights are not permitted. The clothing must have a neckline which does not expose the chest, must not be sleeveless and must be without excessive decoration such as beads, sequins, and the like.

Clothing for Ladies cannot be theatrical in nature. They must have skirts and pants covering the hips and posterior. A unitard is not acceptable. A bare midriff is not acceptable. Clothing must be without excessive decoration such as beads, sequins, feathers, and the like. (USFSA Rulebook 2001, page 146-147)

These guidelines on dress codes sound a little stricter than they really are. Sequins are fine as long they are sure not to come off. Bare midriffs are not permitted, but there is no deduction for skaters choosing skin-colored material around the midriff—for example, if their music is *Scheherazade* or *Samson and Delilah*.

Dreams of Parents

When Anne sees Vicky in her new dress she starts to dream about her daughter as a champion skater. Dreams are fine, but reality is different. Vicky is an adorable little girl with quite some talent, but there is a long and complicated road to becoming a champion skater. It's like a pyramid, broad at the bottom, very narrow at the top.

So, as parents, enjoy how cute your little skater looks—enjoy the moment without further thoughts. The most important thing about skating is not to win the National or World title (i.e., reach the very top of the pyramid), but to enjoy the sport, learn discipline, hard work, good sportsmanship, and coping with unpredictable situations. **Vicky does not skate to become a World champion, but to go as far, and be as good, as *she* possibly can be.** If she achieves this goal she has learned invaluable lessons for later life. If she then also becomes World champion, well that's a great extra bonus, but should not even be thought about at this time.

Taking Care of the Skates

To show off Vicky's red dress the best, she also needs polished skates. Laces should be washed. (Or new laces bought if the old ones look a little worn. You spend so much on skating the odd new laces will not break you.) Dark gray laces spoil any polishing effort. The laces must be well and safely tucked in the boots so there is no chance they will get caught in the hooks of the other boot, causing nasty falls. Parents also should be prepared if laces break and screws come loose. Carry a screwdriver with you as well as a spare pair of laces. Screws really should not come loose; they should be checked the night before a competition. But carry a screwdriver anyway.

Skate Sharpening

Parents of younger skaters should be responsible for their children's skate sharpening, by a competent skate sharpener. Not everybody can sharpen figure skates. Ask your coach where to go for sharpening. Stay with one skate sharpener if he is good. Don't switch around, that can confuse the skater as every sharpener has a slightly different way of "doing skates" (you can use different hollows, but let's not get too technical at this stage). How often should you have the skates sharpened? That depends on how much the child skates, and if the skater is careful to put on skate guards when walking around off the ice. Remind your skaters to put on their guards. They will often forget. All kids do at the beginning. Make it a habit, like brushing their teeth. If a skater wears guards and skates three times a week, I would say every eight weeks is a good time. If a skater skates more, of course you should have the skates done more often. A good sharpening costs between $10 and $20, and helps a lot in producing good and nonwobbly or scratchy edges.

Don't have skates sharpened right before competitions or tests. Sharp skates feel different. Give your skater at least three days to get used to them.

Edges—Their Importance and Beauty

I should really have said blade-sharpening. Blades have two edges. There is a hollow part along the length of the blade. It looks somewhat like an upside down "U" On the sides of the hollow are the two edges. The inside edge is to the inside of the foot and the outside, to the outside. Skaters will often talk about edges and also "flats," meaning that the skater glides on both edges at the same time. Edges are most important in skating. They can be a whole circle, a half circle, or even less, but they are always a curve. These curves help in jumping and spinning, and make ice dancing so special. If it's not a curve, it's not an edge.

Sometimes judges complain about the lack of edges. Especially on moves tests. Wrong edges, or straight or wobbly lines looking more like overcooked or raw spaghetti, then nice curves, can often cause a test to fail.

Things to See to, before Competition

Back to Vicky. It is a good idea to make a list of what to bring to competition. *Hair spray* is important for girls. Neatness counts. Always remember that. **Bobby pins, loose sequins, or anything that can fall on the ice can be dangerous to your skater and to all the ones following her.** Glue the hair together with hair spray. Skaters on Synchronized teams buy nets, put their buns in nets, and then actually sew the buns and net tightly together with fish lines (thin fishing lines used for fishing; they don't show). Just imagine what could happen if 18 or 20 skaters skate, holding onto each other in a

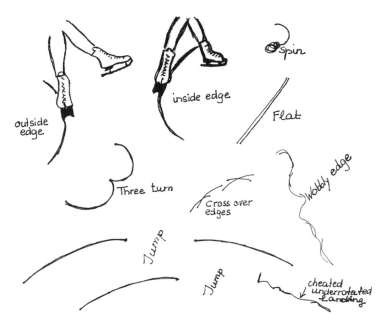

FIGURE 13. On clean ice, white marks which the blades leave on the ice can be seen. When these marks are curved they are called "edges." The skate blade has a hollow, and the strip of metal on either side of it is also called an edge. Due to the flow and the lean of the body, edges are formed. If the edge to the outside of the foot is skated on it is called an outside edge, and if it is to the inside of the foot it is called an inside edge. If both edges of the blades are used together it is called a flat. If skaters have "flats" during a moves test where there should have been edges, the skater is likely to fail. Wobbly lines on the ice where the skater changes edges in an uncontrolled mannner (wavering from the outside to the inside edges) are also frowned upon in skating. This can happen after a jump or during a move—actually anywhere—it nearly always causes a lack of sureness.

very fast circle, and one trips over a bobby pin. Fasten Ponytails with strong double elastic hair bands. If your skaters wear a bun, try it out in practice first to make quite sure it will hold. Bring an extra dress. If the zipper breaks or hot chocolate spills all over the competition dress, you will be so glad you have an extra one. Don't leave it in the car; bring everything into the rink. A spare pair of tights. Pro shops are not always open. Spare laces as well as the screwdriver and the tapes.

What to Eat or Drink before Competition

The following advice is a little exaggerated for a FS-1 skater, but doing it correctly from the start is a good habit to get into. If the competition is midmorning, a normal breakfast: cornflakes, orange juice, toast is fine. A breakfast that is too heavy is not good. Keep carbohydrates high and fats low. Just before competition is not the time to eat. It can cause stomach upsets during the program. A sip of water is fine but not too much of that either. Just to wet the mouth if it feels dry. Of course Vicky should get enough to drink but not immediately before performance. (*No Coke or anything that contains caffeine.*)

There are many good books written on diet. For example: Nancy Clark, MS,RD, *Sports Nutrition Guidebook, Eating to Fuel Your Active Lifestyle*, Second Edition, ISBN 0-87322-730-1; Dr. Michael Colgan, *Optimum Sports Nutrition Your Competitive Edge*, Advanced Research Press, New York, 1993.

Don't Do Things Too Differently Just Because It's Competition Time

A good rule of thumb is to make the time before competition as much as possible like any other day. For example, don't tell Vicky to go to bed at 5:00 the evening before competition to make sure she gets enough rest, when she normally does not go to her room before 9:00. She will only lie awake, stare at the ceiling, and get over-exited about the next day. On the other hand, for older skaters staying over in motels, having parties, running up and down hallways and overstaying their bedtime should be avoided. I suggest a benign television program or even some homework; these things are relaxing.

Talking about Rest in General

Talking about sleep in the previous paragraph brings me to an important point. **If skaters go all out in practice, they do need enough sleep. Ten hours for children is not an exaggeration. Not enough sleep, apart from being unhealthy, makes children listless and irritable.** *Please remember especially if early morning hours are involved in your child's practice.*

Leave Yourself Plenty of Time Driving to a Competition

It will make a skater nervous if the parent drives the car and complains about traffic jams and long red lights and says, "Oh I do hope we'll make it on time." For a young skater it is a good idea to come to the competition rink one hour before performance time. The crush of people, parents, and coaches, milling around can be intimidating enough without the extra tension of too little time to prepare for the event.

SEVEN

The Competition

Anne and Vicky arrive at the competition rink one hour before performance time, and Anne hands in Vicky's performance tape at the registration desk.

Nerves of Parents

The tape had slipped to the bottom of her bag and with trembling hands she fishes it out. Why on earth do her hands tremble? The answer to this is simple—because Anne is nervous. Not for herself but for her child. Most parents are considerably more nervous than their children, especially at the first competitions, and then of course later when a lot is at stake. It is said that Mrs. Flemming kept her eyes tightly closed all through Peggy's Olympic performance. To win the Olympics was, of course, a very big deal for Peggy and no wonder her mother was nervous. Who knows—maybe she wishes now she had seen Peggy's great performance. Why are parents really so nervous? As a parent, one is so helpless. There is absolutely nothing a parent can do once the child has gone out on the ice to start the program. I asked a lot of parents if they knew the reason why they get nervous. I nearly always got the answer, "Because I don't want my child to be sad and disappointed afterward."

I talked to Susie's mom: "Are you nervous because you want your child to win?"

"Oh no, that does not matter to me, but I know how much it matters to Susie, I want her to do well because it will make her so happy. Of course I will be proud of her if she wins, but that's not what is so important to me. What is important is that Susie is happy and pleased with herself, because I know how hard she worked. I hate to see her sad and disappointed. The fear of that is what makes me nervous."

What is important is for parents to try to keep their nervousness from their children. Feelings are "catching." If you say to your skater, "Oh, I am so nervous I don't know what to do," that is a signal to your child that competitions and skating in front of an audience must be frightening. Try to work on yourself. Remember that your children compete because they like it, and therefore take the risk of falling down and messing up the odd program. There is always, as the sports reporter says on TV, "the joy of victory and the agony of defeat." But the children chose to do it so let them—enjoy spending time with them and be positive. Think about how great you and your skater feel when everything went as well as it could, and your child stands on the podium holding a medal or trophy. There is always time to console after a bad performance, but please don't worry about it before it happens.

Result Walls and Starting Orders

Results and starting orders are taped to a wall in the rink building. When results come out, kids push and squeeze and practically fall over each other to see what place they came in. Although at an ISI competition results are simple to read. The first five get placed one through five and the rest are not mentioned, but assumed to be all in sixth place. In USFSA a result sheet is quite a study (see Chapter 15). Often one hears yells of joy, and sees happy children running from the wall holding up one finger to show their parents as quickly as possible that they won. The father of one of my student's, however, seemed to have seen the sad side of the wall. He called this wall the "wailing wall," as bad results can produce tears in kids and killer looks in parents. As a rule, however, one sees many more happy kids than sad ones. Competition organizers want the skaters to return; they are much more likely to return after a good experience. Medals or trophies are often given to the first four skaters. For young skaters to come home with a trophy or medal is often just as important as what place they got.

The Myth of Starting Orders

For Vicky and Anne it is necessary to locate the starting order sheets. Vicky skates fourth. Coaches, if they are around, will often tell the children what number they skate, but often coaches are busy with other skaters and it is the children's responsibility to know their starting order and be ready in time.

Although it is often said that it is bad to skate number one, this really is not so anymore. When a group consisted of 36 skaters, as it did for me at Europeans, then skating first can be a disadvantage. Comparing such a large group is very difficult. The judges can't mark the first skaters too high because they don't know how good a later skater may be. But in a group of 10 or 18 skaters, the judges can go back to the first skater and compare.

However badly you feel as parents about any mishap during competition time, be it starting orders or anything else, don't include the skater in the worries. **A parent's job is to encourage.** If the skater has drawn #1 or #10 makes no difference. Don't say, "Oh great, you skate last." That may be an encouraging statement at the time, but what if your skater skates first at the next competition? It is definitely best to keep quiet and just take the starting order as a fact. Commiserating with the child, saying things like, "Oh you poor thing, you have drawn number one," does not help the skater.

Emotional Changes before Competing

Vicky is unusually quiet and has a tendency to snap at her mother which she normally does not do.

Changes in mood are common in skaters before they perform. Don't take them too seriously; stay calm and avoid getting into a fight with your child before competition however much you feel like strangling them, especially as you, too, get tense during competition time. Anne ignores Vicky's behavior for the time being. She correctly talks to her daughter after the event, when both mother and child are in a calmer mood and Vicky is open to listening. Some skaters told me they just had to snap at somebody to let their worries out before competing. Nobody else would take it except a parent. Vicky, like most children, knows parents forgive and understand. Even so, parents are not punching bags; you should definitely talk about the inappropriate behavior to your children with them.

What to Say to Skaters before They Compete

The loudspeaker announces: "FS-1—six- to seven-year-olds, in the warm-up area please." There goes Vicky with some of her competitors; parents are not welcome in this area even though some sneak in anyway. Anne wonders what to say to Vicky. Just say "**I love you**," that's the best.

If you say, "Skate well !" Vicky may start to worry: What if I don't skate well? If you say: "Do your best!" Vicky may again worry. Of course I'll try, but what if I can't? Even worse: "I still love you, even if you fall 10 times." Will I fall? Vicky really had never thought of that possibility before. Another unfortunate thing to say is the very common, "Don't be nervous!" Vicky *does* feel different than on a normal day. After hearing "Don't be nervous" she thinks that must be nervousness and it is bad. At her young age she probably feels excitement, and anticipation, mixed with a little anxiety. This is called "arousal" in the psychological vocabulary. She wants to go out there and show what she can do. But she does feel different than on a normal day. There is *nothing wrong with this;* on the contrary, that's how it should be.

"Have fun," is another piece of advice parents often give. If Vicky skates well, of course she will have fun. But what if she skates badly?

Knowing her mother loves her is enough for Vicky. She feels comforted and supported. Leave specific advice to the coach. An understanding coach knows the skater better than the best parent when it comes to skating. Frank Caroll knew exactly what to say to Michelle Kwan before she took the ice for her freestyle at World's 2000. He said: "Let it go!" The best parent could not have hit these exact words in that exact tone, at this crucial moment.

Videotaping

It is good to have the performance of your skater video-taped. The whole group is best. One can then look at the tape afterward, sometimes with the help of the coach, and get a better understanding of why the skaters placed where they did. (There is often a professional doing videos, and a tape can be ordered from him.)

Warm-Ups

Before each competition and test there is a warm-up period—when the next group to skate gets a feel for the ice. They are normally between four and six minutes long. It is quite all right to go out in the competition dress, but a tight fitting little jacket over the dress looks good also. Some skaters want to surprise the audience with their outfit at performance time and not show it already in warm-up. For a FS-1 level, just the dress without jacket is quit appropriate.

Parents Should Watch

Yes, of course you should watch. First of all because you can't discuss the performance when you have not seen it; secondly, you want to show your child that you are interested, and not be so unduly nervous that you can't atch. But I was a mother, too. When I competed myself I was excited, but not nervous once I started my program. I was calm when my students skated, but I wanted to close my eyes and hide when my daughters went on. I didn't because I believe it is wrong, but I certainly can commiserate with a nervous parent. Brace yourselves, parents, and watch. Oftentimes you'll get the greatest thrill out of a top performance of your child.

From the time the children go out to warm up until after the performance, parents and friends should stay completely out of the way. There is nothing more irritating for coaches and skaters than if mothers appear with water bottles or last minute unnecessary instructions.

A thing for parents to remember is that in "compulsory events" when the skaters only perform on half the ice, group A often warms up at the same time as group B. One can easily make the mistake of thinking group A is first and group B is second. Be aware of that.

Should Skaters Watch Each Other Compete?

At the FS-1 level it's perfectly fine. Kids learn from each other. However, if a skater does not want to watch, that's okay too. Always take your child's individual needs into account. In more advanced competitions it is better for the skaters not to watch their competitors, until after they have performed themselves. Watching can detract from concentration. It's also very important to keep the muscles moving. Some skaters like to listen to their music with earphones, some others like to listen to their favorite songs also via earphones. Some like to close their eyes and visualize their programs. Whatever works best for the skater is fine. However, to stand stiff and petrified watching the skaters before do a perfect program, should be avoided as well as running around with friends and losing concentration. After the skaters have finished their program, then it is important to watch. Parents be sure and encourage this. It is important for the skater to see what the competition is like. Should the competitors have drawn last to skate, they must then rely on the videotape.

The Performance

Back to Anne and Vicky. The first skater in Vicky's group skates, then another, then yet another, Anne watches attentively. She has to admit that they all skate alike, but maybe the judges will know how to differentiate. Vicky comes on. Anne's mouth feels dry and her hands are clammy. Vicky looks so small in the big rink. Vicky's music begins, and Anne is relieved that nothing went wrong with the tape. Becky stands at the gate, her knees rhythmically bending and straightening with the tempo of Vicky's music. When Vicky does her Spiral, Debbie claps very loudly. Soon it's all over; Vicky curtsies. Anne ιs so happy and sighs with relief. Vicky comes to her Mom grinning. "That was fun," she says. "Was it?" says Anne, hugging her little girl. She does not admit that for her it was quite nerve-wracking.

Soon everybody runs to the wall to see the results. Vicky jumps for joy and screams,

"I got first! Yeah!" At the FS-1 level it is acceptable to scream when you win, but later more quiet behavior is preferable. Good sportsmanship includes understanding that the other children in the group surely also wanted to win as well. They will find a too boisterous behavior of the winner irritating.

A Bad Performance

Vicky Messes Up a Performance

After the first success in competition Vicky increases the level of commitment to her skating. She now has private lessons twice a week, skates four times a week, and both Vicky and Anne quickly learn that one does not win all competitions. However, Vicky normally does very well and displays quite a range of trophies in her bedroom. Having completed the beginning classes and passed FS 1, 2, and 3, Vicky is now in FS-4, where things are getting harder. Still, she seems to have no trouble, gets down in her sit spin and easily understands step sequences. During one FS-4 competition, however, Vicky really does badly. She falls on her sit spin, two foots her loop jump, and gets so flustered that she forgets parts of her program.

As a coach I saw many different reactions from parents after their kids skated badly.

Not all parents behave correctly but all of them love their children, even if their emotions sometimes run away with them. It is always better not to show your feelings in public. Tell your skater to come with you to the bathroom, and not to cry in the crowded lobby. Comfort your child in private away from interested onlookers and skaters who did better.

What to say? It is not a bad idea to be honest and simply say, "I'm so sorry." If it comes from the heart, the children are comforted and relieved that you understand. They are sad and disappointed and it is better to share these feelings without much to-do. Don't go into long explanations that the children don't feel like listening to. The skaters have to come to terms with their bad skate themselves. If the skaters want to be alone, that's fine. If they want to be with you that's just as good. Don't blame anybody. Neither the kid, nor the coach, nor the judges, nor the organization, nor the ice. They just skated badly, that's all. There will be many other better times. Tell the skaters just because things did not work out for them that day, that does not make them a bad skater. Everybody has bad days. When the skaters come off after a disappointing performance normally the Pro takes over. A good coach knows how to handle the skater. Some need support, others need advice on how to improve practice habits, some need a serious talk about their goals, their confidence, etc. Parents have a different job—they are the comforters, they are the "encouragers." It is really hard to know as a parent what form the encouragement should take. There stands your child, tears in the eyes, yet looking extremely irritated with you. You try hugging, but you get pushed away. Ask them, "What would you like me to do?" If the answer is the unfriendly, "Just go away and leave me alone," don't get angry. There is a saying in Switzerland, "Forgive your friend, and try to understand; if he did not feel most miserable himself, he would never hurt you." In this case with your skaters, do what they say—go away. Later on, when things have calmed down, explain that you were hurt, and their behavior was neither helpful to them nor to you. Remember it is their disappointment (you were not the one who skated badly), and it is they who have to cope with it. Try not to be too disappointed yourself, but help your child over this difficult hurdle. You may feel temporarily that your skater did badly to annoy you. That is of course nonsense. You know well that no competitor wants to do badly. It happens due to the unpredictability of the sport.

Arrange a meeting with the coach, the skater, and yourself to discuss training habits. Give the skater ideas of how they can improve themselves. Perhaps they should be more diligent in practicing, not stop the program halfway through if something went wrong, not too much talking with friends during practice sessions, not retie the skates every 10 minutes if it's really not necessary, etc. These are all things over which skaters have control. They have no control if their blade hit a rut in the ice, or the judging was not fair in their view. Skaters have to learn that unpredictable things do happen, that's part of the sport, and the sooner they learn to cope with them the better. As a basic guideline always underline the predictable. It is much more comforting to hear "If you skate better to the music, hold your body up straighter, etc., etc., the judges will give you higher marks." The skater can *do* something about that. The feeling of powerlessness, of being up against something uncontrollable is the worst. I heard a coach tell a student: "Don't worry that you placed badly. The judges just don't know what they are doing." Not much comfort to disappointed skaters, as they have no control over their destiny, neither this time, nor all other competitions to come. They are left in the hands of the judges who don't know what they are doing. As a parent, please avoid blaming the judges. Instead, learn what the judges did not like and why. You can ask your coach to come with you and ask some of the judges, or your coach could go to the judges alone and try to find out. Judges try to be helpful and often will take time to explain. There is only a little part of a thin blade to land the jumps on. A slight body lean can cause a stumble; a bobby pin dropped inadvertently by a previous skater can lead to a bad fall. A lot of skating is not easily controllable. For many children disappointments in achievements don't happen that often. In school if the teacher sees that a student works hard, the child gets rewarded. During a math test they sit on a chair and the only work is with the brain. In competitive swimming they rely 90% on their muscle and breathing powers. Skaters have to listen to their music, remember the footwork, think of jump landings, be artistic and on top of it, smile. Neither a mathematician nor a competitive swimmer have to smile while doing their thing. The reward in skating does not always come when expected. For the last two weeks there was no mistake made in the program, yet in the competition the skaters fall several times. Skaters don't automatically get rewarded for hard work. The child who always goofs around during practice, but does not get at all nervous will sometimes beat the hard worker. So why should any one want to do such a sport at all?

Because the gliding, the speed, the music, the jumps, the spins, make one feel wonderful. The sport has a fascination of its very own. It is the everyday joy of skating that is important. A good competition result is just a well-deserved bonus.

In 1895 George Meager wrote:

I live while I skate; I feel every motion;
all the muscles speak and answer me, as it were,
I talk with my arms, my shoulders, with all
my limbs, and think of music—of flying if you will.

From *The Fine Art of Ice Skating* by Julia Whedon
(Harry N. Abrahams, New York, 1988).

Traps Parents Can Fall into after a Bad Skate

Some parents, due to their own stresses and ambitions, momentarily forget the compassion they all have for their children. Some get so furious that they yell at the child, who already feels lousy. I once saw a mother beat her girl with a skate guard in the parking lot of the rink. I knew how much that mother really loved her daughter. Her emotions just got the better of her. Others take their child in the bathroom and start to scream there. Yet others let their fury out on the Pro. A mother told me: "What kind of Pro have I hired, I wonder. Look how my daughter skated!" The crowning achievement for inappropriate behavior was the mother who tore the result sheet off the wall, crumpled it in a ball, and threw it on the floor. Just imagine how that daughter felt. Then of course there is the well-known car ride home. There the parents have all the time to complain in private, and can really talk themselves into a frenzy. A very understandable, but nevertheless very inappropriate thing to say is, "Look at how much money we are spending for this skating and how many sacrifices in driving and time we are making, and you skate like that." A sentence like this can be remembered much longer by skaters than the parents realize, and come into their minds just before they take the ice for the next competition, with the result that they feel more pressure and get unnecessarily nervous.

Parents have told me, "Yes, I know, I know. . . . I

should be calm, cool, and collected, but I'm human too. It's just so irritating to see Susi make such a mess when I know what she can do." That is a very understandable statement and the only thing I can suggest is that parents can prepare themselves for the eventuality of a bad skate. Skaters are trained and should be trained to think positively. But parents should try to think realistically, know the pitfalls, and not be shocked at a bad skate by their children. It is much better to reprimand children *before* they skate than after. Before, they can change some things for the better. Skating is a very expensive sport and if skaters slack off during practice times, or talk in the lobby or on the ice when they should be skating, *then* is the moment when the parents should clamp down on the behavior. It is quite right if parents scold in the car, on the way home, about that. It is a good idea to ask your skater, *on the way to the rink*, to set some goals for the day's practice. What do they want to concentrate on and what is a good way to go about it. Skaters can definitely do something about practices. All skaters try hard during performance. They may not attack the difficulties correctly, not hold their spins, give up in despair, be out of shape *because of bad practice habits*. But they can't do much about that when performing if they have not practiced correctly. Skaters roughly perform like they practice. Don't expect miracles. Skaters who usually fall six times in their program during practice and only fall five times during performance don't deserve being yelled at for a bad performance. They deserve to be reprimanded in practice. However, some skaters really do get very nervous and then advice of a sports psychologist may help; being furious won't.

More Things Parents Better Not Do

The "overconsoling" parents. Parents can be more disappointed than their children. Hopes may have been unrealistic. They hug their kids and look as if they are at the funeral of their best friend. Even if that skater did not feel too bad after the performance, seeing the sorrow of the parent makes them cry.

Yet another type of parent is the "You have embarrassed me" type. I have heard things like", Now I will not be able to come to the rink for a while; I feel too embarrassed." These parents have not been able to divorce themselves from the skater. This feeling is quite common, but often hard for the parent to realize. Mothers, who probably always would have liked to do something like ice skating but never had the chance, get the glory through their children. And of course the failures. Nobody should feel embarrassed and certainly not the parent.

All these parents who fell into traps during stressful situations at championships are not horrible monsters ill treating their children, they have just lost the perspective of what skating really is all about. We all made many mistakes as parents, and parents of competitive figure skaters have a particularly hard job. The more realistic an attitude parents can have, the better. Practice your attitude toward your child's skating like the children practice their jumps. Try to think every day that skating is your child's thing. It then becomes easier to do the same at competition. If you let yourself dream about your champion skater in the grocery store, check these thoughts to a more realistic attitude. Then you will be more prepared to handle the trying times at competitions, when the child had a bad skate.

A Few Days after a Bad Performance

Vicky loves to skate. Sunday was the day of her bad performance, when tears flowed and her head hung low. On Monday, quite correctly, Anne does not take Vicky to the rink, even though she begged to go skating. By Tuesday, Vicky is her old self again, laughing and jumping and practicing. A bad performance does not diminish her enthusiasm. Maybe Vicky even tries a little harder at practice now. For Anne it's more difficult to get over Vicky's bad skate. What people think affects Anne more, but as she watches Vicky who has forgotten her bad performance, Anne gets things in perspective again. She realizes that she is at the rink to educate and help Vicky in this very special sport she chose, and not to worry about what Monica's mother or any other person thinks about Vicky's bad performance last week.

NINE

The Bleachers, Axels, and Rising Standards

On the bleachers Anne meets a variety of different people watching their children. Some sit engrossed in reading a book, only occasionally looking up or peering over the top of their glasses. But amazingly, they do know exactly what's going on. I never found out how they do it. The gregarious ones talk and laugh and clap when a jump is completed successfully by their child. Some do embroidery with cold fingers; others stay in the lobby and converse there. All of them say, with conviction, that they are just minding their own business. However, everybody seems to know everything about everybody else. Often, driving to and from the rink is too far to make two journeys worthwhile, so these mothers have to stay and watch. Once the skaters get to be teenagers, watching can become stressful for both skaters and parents. If the skaters can drive themselves to the rink or arrange a car pool, all the better. If they cannot drive, interfere as little as ever possible as a parent. Go to the store during sessions, sit in the car and read a book, but don't watch too often. You children just will not like it, however understanding a parent you think you are. One of my students once put it so well: "Mom sitting on the bleachers looks like a sad blackbird ready to descend on her prey."

Parents Should Not Coach

I am writing this subheading so big because I asked many of my coaching friends: "Do you have any advice as to what I should write in this book?" The answer was so unanimous that I felt it was really important, "Do tell them not to teach" . . . so that's what I am doing.

Ideally, watching your skater once a week is enough. Progress of skaters can be slow. Not watching every day can show their improvement better. Whatever you do, don't coach from the bleachers. **Actually, don't coach at all**. I know the temptation to give advice is great, when you sit on these hard benches and watch your child fall again and again. **Still, don't coach.** Trust the instructor. To correct the right thing is difficult and correcting anything will confuse or irritate the skater. If there really is a question about a maneuver, ask the instructor when he or she has come off the ice. Usually the

coach will be willing and helpful in explaining a problem. If skaters need advice they are to ask their teacher in
their next lesson. Don't let them interrupt another
skater's lesson.

The Axel

It is not too long before Vicky passes out of FS-4 into FS-
5. Anne expects her to pass out of FS-5 as quickly as she
progressed from FS-3 to FS-4. But there is a big jump
from FS-4 to FS-5, because FS-5 includes the **Axel**. The
Axel, and later the double Axel, and much much later the
triple Axel are very special. They are all jumps which take
off from the forward outside edge, like one of the very first
jumps a child learns, the waltz jump. The big difference
between the waltz jump and the Axel is the amount of rotation in the air. For most children to rotate half a time in
the air (or not even that much for a waltz jump) is very
easy. To rotate once in the air, like for a Lutz or loop jump,
is not so hard either. But the Axel has one and a half revolutions. That is much harder to do, takes much more practice, and is considered to be a landmark in a skater's
career. Each skater is immensely happy and proud when
the first Axel is landed. I coached for many years but the
thrill of the first Axel of a student never diminished. It's a
big moment. The skaters on the rink often come to a halt
to watch. Nobody would stop for a mere loop jump or

even a Lutz, but the Axel—that's different, and special. Some Pros only take kids after they can do the Axel. The length of time to learn it depends on many things: how good the other jumps are, how much courage and strength the skater has, and of course how it is taught. About a year is a reasonable estimate, although some pupils take longer and some shorter.

Some Names of Jumps and Spins, and How Much More Skaters Achieve Today

Some maneuvers in skating have rather strange names. That is because very often a move or a jump is named after the first skater who did them. Dance turns like Mohawks and Choctaws are named after Indian dances where similar moves were executed.

The Axel is named after Axel Paulsen, who was a Swedish skater. He invented that jump with skates that had no toe picks, which makes it much harder. Skaters know they have to take off for a jump from the ball of the foot, the last thing to touch the ice before they take off being the toe pick. Axel Paulsen had to rely entirely on the ball of his foot on the take-off—he had no toe pick. If the jump had not been named after the inventor it also could be called the double waltz jump, because that is really what it is.

FIGURE 14. Axel Paulsen, the inventor of this famous jump. Do look at his blades—how difficult it must have been to do an "Axel" on these. This photograph was taken around 1890.

Later on, Sonja Henie tried a technically rather incorrect version of the Axel jump. Now most 10 year olds in FS-5 can do it. Sonja took off very round, turning on the ice rather than in the air (that made the one and a half revolutions easier to do). Her free leg swung uncontrolled and wild.

FIGURE 15. Sonja Henie in the midst of her Axel. It shows the wild free leg position now considered incorrect and uncontrolled. In chapter 6 page 55 I stress "make sure the underpants don't show." Look at Sonja's—times change.

FREE LEG POITION BEFORE
AXEL LANDING

THE CROSSED LEG POSITION IN
THE AIR OF TRIPLE JUMPS

FIGURE 16. How the free leg should be held in an Axel and later in the double Axel. The double Axel shows Gus Lussi's idea of the crossed legs in the air. This crossed leg position holds true for the fast rotation in all triple jumps.

Back to names of skating moves. The Camel Spin has nothing to do with a camel (even if some of my students thought one probably had to hunch one's back a lot). It was named after an Australian skater called Miss Campbell who did this spin to perfection in 1937. When the famous coach Gus Lussi saw her spin he said she looked just like a "Lybelli" (a form of elegant dragonfly).

The name just lost it's "p" "b" and "l" due to usage. In Switzerland, where Miss Campbell was not known, this same spin is called "the Balance Spin." The spin is done in the spiral position and balance is very difficult. The American and Olympic Champion Dorothy Hamill invented a variation of the Camel Spin called the Hamill-Camel.

The "Shoot the Duck," a move many young children love because they can fall and slide afterward without hurting themselves, has many different names. In America it was felt that skaters doing Shoot the Ducks looked like guns ready to shoot ducks. In Switzerland, a rather military nation, it's called the "Cannon" and in England, appropriately for a country where people love tea, it's called the "Teapot."

"The Spiral" (Vicky's prize move) is called the "Swallow" in Switzerland because the hands are extended a little like a bird's wings. In Austria that same maneuver is called the "Little Angel," again beca▉▉▉ the wings. "The Lutz" was first performed by Aloi▉ I could go on with examples but it would become boring. The thing to remember is that if you▉ funny name in skating it is probably named af▉ skater who invented that move.

What some students
think a Camel Spin with
a "hump" like a camel
should look like.

The real
Campbell spin, now
spelled Camel spin,

FIGURE 17. Camel Spins performed by a skater of the Darien Sportsplex in Darien, Illinois.

Falling can
be fun.

FIGURE 10 Some "Shoot the ducks," or "Cannons" or "Teapots"
performed by skaters of the Darien Sportsplex, Darien, Illinois.

FIGURE 19. A Spiral, or "Little Angel" or "Swallow." The same name for this beautiful move, performed by a skater of the Darien Sportsplex, Darien, Illinois.

Rising Standards. Skaters Do More and More Difficult Things

Skating technique has changed so much. Nearly every year we see the difficulties increasing. What was considered impossible in the time of Sonja Henie is now thought of as easy. Axel Paulsen considered his jump a great achievement and now it is tripled in men's world class competition. Why has the difficulty risen so? One answer is the push of wanting to be the best. If one skater wins with a single jump the next competitor will try that jump double in order to overtake his rival. Then the next skater will try the jump triple and so on and so on. Are skaters going to do sextuples in a few years? Better equipment, more ice time (due to so many more indoor rinks), a better understanding of body movement, all help in increasing the difficulty to higher and higher levels. A big question which keeps on being raised is the increased injury rate at the top levels. We all have to admit that for some skaters triple jumps are very difficult. But these skaters know that without triples they are not competitive. So they try and try until a bone is stress fractured. Coaches, parents, and definitely also skaters themselves have to know when enough is enough. Three hours per day of jumping may result in landing the odd triple, but also most probably—I think one can say surely—will result in injury. Flowing edges, moves in the field, spins, and dance steps should fill two hours if a skater is on the ice for three. Concentrated skatin two hours per day is often sufficient. Skaters should spend enough time on off-ice strengthening and ballet. They should be trained to tell their parents and coaches when something hurts. Off course there is always a golden mean. Some skaters may be constantly ailing and have to learn to endure a little pain, others only finally admit to an injury when the stress fracture has happened. Should we go on pushing these very difficult jumps? That is an often debated question and no clear answer has been found. Yes, the presentation mark in the long program is the decisive mark. What that means is: should there be a tie, the presentation mark beats out the technical mark. But if a skater has three triple jumps in her program and her competitor has none, the technical mark is so much higher that a tie does not occur. Did skating lose beauty through all these triples? If they are well done, so well that they flow and explode and fit in musically, no, I really don't think so. When Michelle Kwan does her triple triple combination it looks so easy one wonders why she sometimes does not do it. We have seen programs like that. For example the Russian and World Champion 2001 Evgeni Plushenko skated a beautiful program this season with quadruple jumps and yet with a lot of artistry, and so did his rival the other Russian, Alexei Yagudin. However, what happens a lot is that skaters try jumps which are too difficult for them because they know without them they cannot do as well as ᵧy would want to. Often the result is unfortunate, the ᵃ am is flawed with several falls, the jumps are "telegraphed" (meaning that the skater hesitates and waits a long time before attempting to jump), so that everybody can see: "Ah, here comes the jump . . . let's cross our fingers" . . . and down falls the skater. Parents, have you got an answer to this question?

Vicky's Axel Troubles

Back to Vicky. Anne watches with amazement that something that looks so easy when others do it can be so difficult for her daughter. Vicky slips, falls, gets up, tries again, and just can't get that extra half turn in the air. She spends nearly all of her lesson time on Axels and preparations for it. Skaters need lots of practice, and parents need **lots of patience**. We often say skating is a sport of repetition. One hundred or two hundred tries is not enough to master a difficult jump, let alone get it consistent. A thousand times is closer to reality. A jump can be "walked out" and split into it's component parts. Parents often wonder what their child is doing, just lifting her leg without even jumping, or spending a lot of time holding on to the barrier, trying to do parts of the jump. Trust the coach and don't wonder too much. Sometimes the whole lesson may be given off- ice for a particular jump. Sometimes a whole lesson is given on the harness.(When the skater is strapped into a harness, with the coach skating up and down the arena holding the harness by a rope, it helps the skater feel the lift of jump and works on the weaker parts.) If your child is persistent, your coach knows what he or she is doing the Axel will be learned.

Anne watches day after day, and at least to her eyes, the same attempt is made over and over again without much improvement. She hears the coach say, "Very good Vicky; that was much better," as Vicky sits down on the ice after an attempted Axel. "If she fell, what can be so much better about it?" thinks Anne. A jump can be a much better attempt, even if the landing fails. A cheated (underrotated) jump where the skater stands up may not be as good as a fully rotated jump and a fall. Parents will learn to see the difference after a while. The main thing, is not to get impatient. Don't ask Vicky too much about this Axel, especially during the car ride home. Vicky may well be frustrated too. Give her as much encouragement as possible. Remind her that the Axel takes all skaters a long time to learn. Tell her she will land it. Many people before her have learned it, and many after her will do so as well. Try not to compare your children with other skaters with the well-meant intention to make them work harder.

"Look at Susan, what a nice Axel she has," is sure to irritate and discourage your skaters. It will hardly ever make them work harder. The coach may have someone demonstrate the Axel for the student, but the coach will not compare the skaters. The demonstration is just to ꭼmphasize a particular part of the jump.

Coaching Problems

Do Not Believe Everything You Hear in the Bleachers

One afternoon as Anne is sitting in her usual bleacher spot, another skating mom plunks herself next to her. "Still working on the Axel"? says Emma, Monica's mother with glee.

"Yes, it's hard for Vicky," replies Anne.

"Oh it's hard for most skaters you know; my Monica learned it in a week, but then, she has a very good Pro," brags Emma. Don't be too quick to believe all you hear from other parents. More than likely Emma did not know what an Axel was until Monica showed her when she could do it. Or Emma just sees Monica's skating through rose-colored glasses. It had to have taken long than one week to learn an Axel, especially for the r~ plump little Monica. Apart from Monica learn¹

Axel so quickly, something else bothers Anne. It was when Emma said, "But then she has a very good Pro." There are skating instructors, and Pros. Both are called coaches; Pros usually teach the more advanced skaters. Vicky has a skating instructor, Monica has a Pro—is that right? Maybe Vicky should have a Pro and not a skating instructor? If doubts occur it is better for parents not to ignore them. Discuss the questions together at home and over the phone with other skating parents. (Don't do this on the bleachers; the walls around any bleachers of any ice rink "have ears.") Ask the skaters how they feel. In Vicky's case she is very young, and her answers might be somewhat immature. There is more than one reason Anne has doubts about Debbie's suitability as a teacher for Vicky. Becky is mainly a skate-school instructor. Is she really qualified to teach an Axel? Seeing Vicky struggle day after day is frustrating for Anne. Becky has taught the other jumps very well. Vicky does a beautiful high and fast Lutz, a good loop, and nice spins. So why should Becky not be able to teach an Axel? She may well be able to, but very few of her students are advanced enough to do an Axel. It is not bad to judge coaches by their students. If a coach has a majority of very good students, she most likely knows how to teach. Becky teaches mainly beginners. That does not mean she can not teach an Axel, but she has not much ʳperience in comforting and explaining to Anne that ᵈles occur for every skater. The Axel just happens to ᵏy's first one.

Has My Skater Enough Talent?

Let's go back to Emma, who is still talking in the bleachers.

"When are you switching Vicky into USFSA?" (See Chapter 2.) "You know," continues Emma, "if you really want good competition, that leads higher and higher; you'd want Vicky to skate USFSA. Monica does both ISI and USFSA at this moment, but soon she will skate only USFSA." Why has Becky never asked her about USFSA? Anne wonders. Has Vicky not enough talent?

That is not why Becky has not asked, but most parents worry about the talent issue. Let's try and define the word talent:

1. *An ability to learn and grasp skating maneuvers easily, including the ability to lift in a jump. Vicky can certainly do that. (Never mind the Axel problem.)*
2. *To be artistic and musical. Vicky is definitely musical and artistry cannot really be judged at her age.*
3. *The ability to glide and flow with ease across the ice. Yes, Vicky can do that also.*

So it's pretty clear Vicky has enough talent.

But to make a good skater, talent is only a part of a much bigger whole. Will Vicky continue to work hard and be patient if some jump causes her great difficulty? How will her body change in the teenage years? Will her enthusiasm stay with her? Will she be able to take disappointments? Will she have enough patience to deal injuries? Will she be able to give up extra curri tivities at school in order to skate? Nobody knows yet if Vicky has all these qualities. At the moment Vicky is enthusiastic, loves to skate, and works hard. That surely is a good start. If the inevitable increased cost does not become an impossible financial burden for the rest of the family, all Vicky needs is support and opportunity. She will certainly not only learn how to skate, but get lots of valuable education as well. A few bad placements at competitions, a jump which causes difficulty, are a very important part of learning tenacity and discipline. Don't think, "Is it all worth it? Will my daughter ever get somewhere in competition?" If the Olympics is the idea of getting somewhere, then that's not looking at the sport correctly. To skate as a special joy in one's life should be the goal. If Vicky dreams of the Olympics, by all means let her—don't destroy her dream. But parents should be realistic. The Olympics is a great but unlikely goal. What should be the goal is having your skaters achieve their personal best. Give them as much opportunity as you can. The goal could be to take skating very seriously, or to skate for recreation.

Coaches Dream Too

That Becky has not asked Vicky to join USFSA has nothing to do with talent. It has to do more with Becky herself. Becky does not feel comfortable with USFSA and to teach ISI. Her ambition is to become director of the skate-school program, not to develop champions. And even though Becky does not really like teaching USFSA and knows Vicky may one day switch, Becky sees Vicky's ability and does not want to give her up to another coach. Vicky, in Becky's most fantastic dreams, may make the Olympics, and she, Becky, would sit in the famous "kiss and cry" area, having turned miraculously into a USFSA coach. She would be on national TV. Not only skaters and mothers dream—coaches dream sometimes, too.

Conflicting Advice

Let's go back for a third time to that afternoon where Emma has been bragging to Anne about her Pro and her USFSA participation. Emma has to "run" (she's always in a hurry), this time to an off- ice class for Monica. As soon as Emma leaves the bleachers Anne sees a welcome figure. Here comes Mary. Anne smiles invitingly at Mary to sit next to her. Anne likes Mary. "Well, well, and how's life?" asks Mary, holding a bag of popcorn.

"I'm a bit confused," confesses Anne.

"Let me see, Vicky's Axel, or better said, non-Axel, bothers you," guesses Mary.

"Yes, that's part of it; the other part is the USFSA business."

"So they are already trying to get you really volved, eh? Take my advice—stay out of it. It is ve pensive. My Stacey is strictly ISI and skates twice a week or so. It took her years to get the Axel, but what does it matter? She has fun. I have two other children and we want to go on vacation sometimes, too. You can't do everything you know. I just like Stacey to have fun, that's all, and not pull my hair out with worry."

This is a perfectly reasonable and sensible view, only it does not really encourage skaters to excel, and become the very best they can be. It is fun, and it is very good exercise—that is the good thing about skating, there are many more ways than one to get something out of it.

If Anne was confused before, after the talk with Mary she is completely bewildered. She asks Vicky on the way home, "Do you know what USFSA is?" Anne gets the immediate reply: "Oh yes, Mom, that's a fun competition where you get to sleep in a motel." "I see", responds Anne, "who told you?" "Oh, the kids." "But you'll have to skate a lot more if you do USFSA competitions." "Oh fun, yeah!" is the answer Anne gets. If $10,000 is not too much of a financial burden, then by all means let Vicky join USFSA. If budgeting $10,000 is more difficult but still possible and Vicky is really enthused and so are you, then continue but with the knowledge that things get more expensive as you progress in the sport. Both parents working, as said before, is one solution to a better financial situation. In Vicky and Anne's case, both parents agree to give her the chance.

The Grouping of Skaters. How Much Money Will Be Involved?

I have roughly divided skaters into three groups. Let us be quite clear from the beginning of this chapter that these groups are only to be looked at as guidelines. A lot of overlap can occur; i.e., skaters can change their commitment, take the sport much more seriously or much less seriously, and therefore change from one group into the other.

"The Recreational Skater"

Skaters just skating for fun. Not that skating should not be fun for all, but these skaters have less commitment and less investment in the sport. They skate twice three times a week, and maybe join an ISI Synchro team. Their ambitions are limited to taking some ISI tests and participating in some ISI competitions, and doing the annual Ice Show. The budget can be set by parents more easily. If one private lesson a week is all the budget can be stretched to, that skater can still compete for the rink and not feel disadvantaged. The cost of skating does not rise substantially with higher ability levels. I would say $9,000 per year or even less would be a fair estimate. Some skaters opt to test USFSA and otherwise stay in ISI, which is one of the many choices skaters have. Of course this will increase the cost.

"The Serious Skater"

These athletes skate five times a week, take their USFSA tests, participate in quite a number of USFSA Nonqualifying Competitions, and compete at the Regional Championships. They may well become part-time teachers for skating schools. They have a good clean hobby which keeps them out of trouble and gives them lots of joy. Parents also can increase lesson times, engage choreographers, and go to music cutters. But the commitment is not as great as for the committed competitor.

Note, parents, don't feel locked in and think: "Now that I have committed to a "Serious Skater" my child has to stay in this group forever." If it turns out that your child really improves by leaps and bounds, you can always change into the "Committed Competitors" Category.

"Committed Competitors"

These skaters often have reduced school schedules to enable them to skate when the rinks are less crowded and the coaches have more time. Their ambition is to make it further than Regionals, possibly Nationals and hopefully some International competitions.

A big question: At what age do you decide which group your child should go into?

If you wait too long your child may be too old to join the "Committed Competitor" group. If you make up your mind when your children are six years old and you decide to make them a "Committed Competitor," they have really very little say. They are just pushed into skating and won't really have the time or opportunity to think of anything else.

In my opinion there is a lot of overlap between the "Serious Skater" and the "Committed Competitor." If you want your children not to "miss the boat" and still not completely engross themselves in the sport, my advice would be to go into the

"Serious Skater" Category. From there it is not such a big step either way. In other words, start in the middle if your budget allows it.

An Interview with a Mother of a Would-Be "Serious Skater"

Her child is eight years old. It's young to make such a commitment, yet time passes quickly in skating. St young will be of great advantage to the skater. By waiting too long the skater may lose valuable time. Parents agonize a little . . . should we? Should we not? If your children are enthused enough and push you day in, day out, to drive them to the rink, that helps in deciding. If after a few years it becomes clear the child does not want to skate that much, you may all be happier if they change to the "Recreational Skater" group.

"What will it all cost?" asks the mother.

"A lot."

"Isn't that a bit vague?"

"Sure."

"Can you be more specific?"

"What goals do you and your skater have?"

"She *wants to go to the Olympics; I want her to go as far as she can."*

"What level is she at?"

"USFSA Pre-Pre Test and ISI FS-4. She skates four times a week."

"What are you spending at the moment?"

"I don't really count it up—it's too scary, but I would say around $900 a month, not counting new boots and blades. Grandma bought those."

"Do you have a feeling that the expenses for skating won't stay at this level as your daughter advances?"

"I guess so."

"It's not too hard on this budget at the moment for you?"

"Well, no, not really,."

"Does your daughter like to skate?"

"She simply loves it. She lost some competitions and won some. The thing is, she really truly set her heart on skating."

I would say that for a competitive Pre-Pre tester one can get away with $8,000 or $9,000 a year, depending on how much they skate and how many lessons they take. In my opinion there is no difference at this early stage of Pre-Pre Tester and Pre Tester between a "Serious Skater" or a "Committed Competitor." Should your skater stay in the "Serious Skater" Category for their entire career you may well get away with $15,000 to $30,000. Hopefully, up to the senior level.

For Pre-Juvenile and Juvenile skaters who really are aspiring to become a "Committed Competitor," I believe $15,000 to $25,000 would be a reasonable estimate. If the skaters compete seriously and go to Regionals. If they place in the first four at Regionals they will go on to Junior Nationals and things will get more and more expensive. But I strongly advise that parents of young beginning skaters should take it **step-by-step.** If your skater qualifies for Junior Nationals, somehow you will find a way. Don't worry about the expenses of Junior Nationals before the child has even qualified.

If you decide to go into the "Committed Compe~~~ tor" category then things do get more expensive ability level. For an Intermediate skater $15

$30,000 is not unrealistic. Novice then would rise from $30,000 to $40,000+ if many out of town competitions are involved, as well as expensive choreographers and possibly some out of town training.

As I was talking, I saw the stunned look of this mother. It was mind-boggling to her how I threw around the thousands of dollars without flinching an eyelid. But remember, go step-by-step. With your eight-year-old Pre-Pre Tester you are not at a competitive Novice expense level. You are in the "Serious Skater" category. There is time to decide, depending on how the child does, if the enthusiasm stays, etc.

Forms of Support Other Than from Parents

The Memorial Fund

Most skaters don't really know the history of the Memorial Fund. I will never forget it. I was in England at the time (1961). I stood on the ice teaching when a colleague came on the ice saying, "Oh my God, the American skaters crashed in Belgium." It was such a shock to all of us. The whole skating team, plus officials—gone. In memory of this accident the Memorial Fund was created. "The underlying thought in the establishment of Fund was to create a living and continuing memorial 1961 World Team that would be of assistance to spiring skaters" (*Rulebook*, 2002, page 261). A skater with exceptional talent and very limited financial means can get assistance through the Memorial Fund. However, these skaters must have shown excellent competitive results and have potential in National and International competitions.

Very gifted skaters also may find a sponsor. Perhaps a well-known coach has taken an interest in these skaters and personally knows some sponsors. Keep in mind these **are the very few exceptions.**

It is a big decision if the choices fall between college money and skating. As said before, don't jeopardize the family well-being. Do not take college funds saved for other siblings and spend them on the maybe-champion. If the skaters want to forgo college for a while and then later on put themselves through college, that is a possibility. Not all skaters want to become skating coaches or Show skaters to earn a living. They may want to consider a different profession later. Don't let them regret having not gone to college, especially because skaters often have an easier time in college than the average students since they have already learned what commitment, discipline, and organizing their time is all about.

How Do You Make the Decision in Which Group the Skater Should Go?

The first rule is the children have to love skating even if they are still very young and the parents are the decisio makers. When the children grow older they have to cide between giving up school activities like join baseball team, taking part in a school play, becoming a cheerleader—or skating. With the time commitment skating takes, outside school activities often have to be crossed off the list.

Then comes the financial aspect. If it is really too hard on the rest of the family and would cause undue hardships I would advise : don't do it. Once you have started your skaters in the "serious skating" program and they do well, it can be heartbreaking for you and the skaters if you have to stop because financially there is just no way.

If You Made the Decision to Take Skating Seriously There Are Still Ways to Save

Where Can You Save?

Get a Cheaper Coach?
Possibly the cheapest in the rink, who is not much better than the skaters themselves?

Answer: **NO.**

Because a good experienced coach can teach the child faster. What takes the inexperienced coach four lessons to explain, the more knowledgeable coach can often do in one. Also if a bad habit is created it can take much ⊃nger to unlearn than to do it correctly in the first place.

ʰe Least Expensive Boots and Blades?
: NO

If a ready-made boot fits the skater well, there is no need to get the much more costly custom boots, but the skates **really have to fit well**. A lot of money can be saved in bills for foot doctors if your skater has a correctly fitting boot. Also improvement can be slower if the boots give problems. A knowledgeable skate fitter is very important.

Can Skaters Save on Free Skating Sessions
If They Use Them Wisely?
Answer **YES**.

What Is a Good Practice Session and How Can You Help Your Child with This?

Part of learning how to skate is also to learn how to practice without supervision. For many children this is a new form of learning, as most children are supervised most of the time. Maybe skating could be compared to learning a musical instrument, where the practice at home is also mostly done without supervision.

How hard is "hard work" on a day-to-day practice session? For younger skaters as well as teenagers, practices can be rather listless. Proper warm-up is a vital part for practices. (Don't just hang around the lobby talking to your friends; do something constructive, jump rope, run around the lobby, etc.) If skaters warm up well before going on the ice—so well that they get hot and take off their sweaters (raise their body temperature by one degree)—the skaters easily save 15 minutes of very costly ice time. They don't have to warm up on the ice; lobby time is free. Hardworking skaters get away with two freestyles some days, when others have to take three for the same amount of work done. (A note for drivers: In order to warm up correctly, be at the rink at least 20 minutes before the free skating session starts. If the school does not permit this, well then warming up on ice does become a necessity and this money can't be saved.) Too many sessions taken per day are actually a waste of money because skaters cannot, and do not work hard for four hours in a row. Taking that many sessions will get skaters used to slacking off because they are too tired. Unfortunately, what does not work is the theory that if Mary takes three sessions and my Elly takes four, Elly will beat Mary in competition.

Everybody can figure out how much ice time is wasted if skaters are regularly five minutes late. A typical freestyle costs $9 or $10 for 45 minutes. Let's say $8; that would be roughly 17 cents a minute. For five minutes it's 85 cents. You can figure out on your own how much will be saved by not being late.

Let's watch one of those rather miserable practice days. Skaters get on five minutes late. They stroke half-heartedly, do a jump, then talk, then retie their skates, then hang at the barrier, then get off five minutes before the session is over. Can you count how much time and therefore money they wasted?

Of course parents should motivate and encourage their children to work hard. But I have yet to see a parent who will discourage hard work with the ice time being so expensive. What could you do as parents? First of all, expect to see your skater working when you watch and come into the rink at different times and sit on different parts of the bleachers. Again, most skaters work harder, or at least feign as if they work harder, when parents are watching. They may practice 20 easy jumps, wildly circling around and around, which looks like hard work to the parents but is really not very productive. There are certain things parents really can judge. If the program is played, the skaters must not stop or leave out elements. That every parent can see. If the program is done half-heartedly they should reprimand their children. Talking with other skaters (even if they say they were talking about jump theories) should not be condoned. They can talk about jump theories in the lobby when the session is over. It can be helpful if parents videotape their skaters during practice. Parent and skater can look at the tape at home and make suggestions on how to improve practice habits. As a parent, don't criticize the technique; that's the coaches' job. Videotape a specific move and then let the skaters comment on what could be improved. Maybe they never noticed how slow they went, how much they leaned forward, and if your video has good sound—how much they scratched instead of glided.

Another Way to Save Money:
Give Them a Break Once in a While

Take a break once in a while. When I was training we did not have ice all year. That made us keener to practice when we could. Apart from saving money, skating without a break all year round can burn the skater out. Discuss with your coach which are the best times for breaks.

Get Job

Sometimes mothers can get jobs as ice monitors at rinks and get a few sessions free for their child. Other mothers can sew really well and can make extra money by sewing skating outfits. Sometimes Pro shops have openings in the rink. These are only a few suggestions. Don't get a job where driving your child to and from the rink becomes a problem; that would defeat the purpose.

How Much Ice Time?
How Much Off-Ice Training and Ballet?
How Many Lessons?

Ice Time

First of all, a lot depends on what your coach suggests. Secondly, it depends on what level your skater is (see Test Level in Chapter 2). Less ice time is needed for a Pre-Preliminary skater than for a Senior. A Pre-Preliminary to Preliminary can get away with one 45-minute freestyle three times a week and two 45-minute freestyles the other two days. Up to Intermediate two 45-minute freestyles five times a week during the school year is a good number in my opinion. Three 45-minutes would be adequate from Novice on up; however, many Novices and even Junior skaters can get away with taking two freestyles if they work very hard on them and are not late. (By working very hard I don't mean "jump-jump-jump"; that will almost certainly cause injuries, but work intelligently and thoroughly. In the summer, when training is at its height, a stroking, moves and ice dance class added on different days is a good supplement. Summer skating usually is about eight to ten weeks of rigorous training. But again, it could be that your coach has a different schedule in mind. Skaters can divide each freestyle doing jumps for half the time and the other half moves, spins, and steps of the program. Another option would be to jump on one freestyle and not jump on the other two. However the skaters and coaches want to divide it.

Off-Ice?

As a general rule, one might say five hours off-ice to ten hours on ice. Again, this may vary depending on the coach, the level of the skaters, etc. But skaters do need some off-ice training. It is much more important than many people understand. Off-ice training includes ballet and strength training, flexibility training, and maybe for more advanced skaters, some theater expression classes. Of course all these classes cost money too, and sometimes parents just have to economize. But here a warning is in order—don't economize on strength and flexibility training, as this is an important part of injury prevention.

How Many Lessons?

How much do coaches charge? This of course is a very individual matter. Some famous world coaches may well charge over $120 per hour. Some Master rated coaches with students at National level can be around $90 per hour, and good lesser rated Pros may charge $80 per hour on down. A skating school instructor teaching a little beginner might charge only around $60 an hour.

What coach you choose for your skater is both very important and not easy. Watch how they teach and what relationship they have with their students. Are the students good?

It is unlikely that a very mediocre teacher would have a lot of first-class skaters. Look up the PSA ratings; ask around. Find out from other parents who their children take lessons from and how pleased they are. If you are spending a lot of time and effort to educate your skater, don't save on coaches' lesson fees. If you found a coach who meets your needs in every way except that he or she is very expensive, try to overcome this hurdle unless it is really out of range.

How many lessons? Let's presume you found a good coach and he or she suggests four lesson a week, 20 minutes each, and one lesson on moves. If you can afford that, I think it is a very good beginning up to the Juvenile or Intermediate level. Later on, the lessons will increase. There will be lessons on Moves, possibly by a dance coach; lessons on choreography by a choreographer; maybe lessons from another helping coach, etc., etc. Most mothers I have interviewed have told me that ice time was very expensive, but that lesson time was the most costly.

TWELVE

The Change of Coach

The day after the USFSA decision for Vicky has been made, Anne meets Becky by the snack bar. Anne opens the conversation with the usual mother question: "How is Vicky doing"?

"Oh fine, the Axel will come. I must rush—I have another lesson," says Becky, as she disappears through the doors leading into the rink. Anne had not expected a long explanation of the differences between ISI and USFSA plus the prophecy of great achievements in the future for Vicky, but she had expected a little more than "fine." Becky does not really have to rush, but she does not want to talk to Anne just now. She feels bad about Vicky's Axel and has not had sufficient experience to know what to say to parents of children at the "axel-trouble-stage," so she takes flight before she has to explain too much. Anne begins to feel that maybe a coach change would be in order.

She learns about PSA ratings (see Chapter 2). She is starting to look at how coaches teach, the students they have, how Vicky may fit in with a particular group.

Rink Atmosphere

At Vicky's rink Helena is the top Pro. Some of her students make it to Nationals most years. Not all rinks have competitive programs at that high a level. Only by chance did Anne find this very competitive rink on that rainy Sunday she took Vicky skating for the first time. If you have a skater who wants to compete seriously, it is a good idea to look around the area and find a rink with a strong competitive program. Some rinks are primarily recreational, some are mainly hockey, and others cater mainly for park district demands. It is interesting what "atmosphere" does. Many skaters will improve just seeing, or if possible, skating with more advanced students. There is an unwritten law: "What they can do, I can do too." To be with better skaters is often very advantageous.

However, if parents and skaters are happy where they are skating, and satisfied with the progress, do not start to think, "The grass is greener on the other side." Some skaters progress better if they feel they are one of the best in their rink. They feel more confident and not threatened by better and sometimes a little "uppity" skaters. As the saying goes, "If it's not broken, don't fix it." If you are happy where you skate, stay there.

Observe Skating Coaches

Anne makes a special trip to watch Helena teach. She teaches at 1:00 in the afternoon. (Anne wonders at what time her students go to school.) She is wearing a long coat and moves very slowly around the ice. Students in lesson come up to her after each jump or maneuver they are doing. Anne is impressed with the jumps they are trying. There are also some excellent young boys skating. It is astonishing that all of them fall so much. Anne thought Vicky fell a lot, but it is nothing compared to what she is seeing now. Anne wonders if this a good thing for her little girl to do, if it involves so much falling. Relax—these skaters have fallen so much that they have learned how to fall without hurting themselves. Of course injuries do occur, but when learning a jump and therefore expecting to fall, most skaters don't hurt themselves much. It's the unexpected fall that can hurt more, catching a gouge in the ice or bumping into another skater sometimes can cause nasty injuries.

The session Anne watches is obviously for the most advanced skaters. One girl in particular impresses Anne. She skates so gracefully to her music. Could Vicky ever learn to skate like that? There are not as many mothers sitting on the bleachers as during Vicky's skating sessions. This is because some of these skaters are old enough to drive themselves to the rink, or have arranged for car pools.

Anne asks who that musical skater is and hears that she has made it to Nationals. The boy who spins like a top and does jumps with so many rotations has even earned a spot at World's.

"I have a little girl who skates too," says Anne, "but she is still very young. Only seven, to be exact."

"Do you know what you have let yourself in for?" asks one of the mothers.

"Not really," replies Anne.

It is very difficult to know. One learns mainly just by going on day by day and step by step. Not all parents' experiences will be the same. All parents should be admired for the sacrifices they make to skating and the love they have for their children, going through joys and hardships with them.

Anne Asks Helena about Teaching Vicky

There is never any harm in asking, but Helena has very advanced students. The needs of advanced students and so-called "little kids" are different. Helena is often away at competition. She has to go to international competitions, this year even to Worlds. Even though Helena has a helping coach (a former student of hers who wants to go into teaching), the helping coach will be very busy too, when Helena is gone.

Helena comes off the ice, still busily discussing a music problem with one of her students. Anne is a little hesitant but decides to go ahead.

"Would you take a seven-year-old for lessons?"

"A seven-year-old? That's very young. What can she do, and when does she skate?"

"Four times in the late afternoon, and the Axel gives her problems; apart from that she skates well, and has done very well in ISI competitions."

"I have very little time at the moment, and my assistant will be very busy too when I am gone. I really don't take students before they have a good strong Axel and a double Salchow. What I suggest," continues Helena, "is that you ask somebody like John. He was a very good skater himself, made it to Nationals and has just started teaching at our rink. If later on in your daughter's career you need more advice I will certainly be glad to talk to you and watch your daughter skate."

Anne really knew that Helena is not the coach for Vicky at the moment, but that she was so willing to give advice and take an interest in Vicky's progress was encouraging.

John has "Senior Free Style "and "Senior Moves" in PSA ratings (the second highest ratings). He does teach USFSA, takes students to Regionals, and has had the odd pupil at the Sectional level. Anne has already watched him teach on the sessions Vicky skates, and found his students looked happy and enthused. He seems responsible, on time, and conscientious with his lessons.

Anne decides to ask John. She catches him just as he is about to go on the ice. Anne asks about taking Vicky on for lessons.

"Sure thing; can she come in the mornings? Afternoons I'm booked."

"But Vicky has school in the mornings."

"Oh, I mean I have still some openings at 6:00 a.m. It's not that crowded then."

"No wonder," thinks Anne.

"I've seen your little girl skate, she is cute; quite some talent I think." Anne is happy that John had already noticed Vicky, and says she will talk to him about lessons soon. She has not talked to Becky yet and that comes first. John understands and seems really interested.

"Pro Hoppers"

Anne has no intention of becoming a "Pro hopper." There are skaters who run from Pro to Pro, blaming the lessons they are getting, rather than their impatience with slow progress, or inability to take failure. If Vicky wants to become more serious with her skating, changing coaches is justified. But once a compatible coach is found, expect some disagreements, some complaints from Vicky, and even some tears if things don't go right. Discuss problems with your coach by all means, but don't just switch. It normally does not help. I remember a famous skater who won Nationals once. She was asked by a reporter about a Pro she had worked with three years previously.

"Oh, you mean who I worked with three years ago? Then I was on Pro number seven. Now I am on number eleven." She is an extremely talented skater, but her performances have become rather inconsistent, one day on, one day off. Unreliable performances can happen to anybody; however, a steady relationship with a coach can help a skater to stay on a more even keel.

THIRTEEN

Skating is Getting More Serious for Vicky

What Vicky Thinks about Changing Coaches

Anne correctly feels Vicky ought to be involved in the change of coach, so she asks, "Would you like to take lessons from someone else?"

"Why?" asks Vicky, very surprised. "Is it because I can't land my Axel?"

"Of course not, (a little white lie perhaps?) but I thought you would like to compete in USFSA and Becky does not teach any USFSA skaters."

"Who would I take from?"

"I talked to John, do you know who I mean?"

Vicky gets really exited, "Oh John, yes he's nice, yes O.K. Will Becky be sad? But maybe he can help me with my Axel?"

The Axel seems to be more important to Vicky than Becky's possible sadness. The affair is settled for Vicky. That attitude of Vicky is not untypical of a very competitive child. It is good in many ways, but, as parents, also teach your children gratefulness and understanding for the coach you are leaving.

How to Change a Coach. First the Unpleasant Things

Brrr, Anne shudders. Anne hates hurting anybody's feelings, and certainly Becky's, who has been so nice to her little girl.. "Maybe I should just leave things the way they are. Less money, less agonizing as Mary had said" (Chapter 8) But realizing that it is too late now to reconsider, Anne calls Becky and arranges to meet her. Anne could just have told Becky over the phone, but Becky had tried so hard with Vicky, was always so nice, she deserved more than a phone call. What do you say as a parent to the coach you are leaving? Anne starts off with thanking Becky for all she has done for Vicky. She praises Becky's feeling for children and her patience with Vicky. Then she goes ahead and tells her what the meeting is about. She does not prolong the agony by talking about trivia. Anne well knows that Becky will not like what she is hearing, so it's better to get it done and over with.

"My husband and I" (how good it was that Anne could blame Paul a bit), "would like Vicky to compete in

USFSA and we have decided to change coaches." Becky is hurt; she does not want to lose Vicky—she really likes that little girl. But Becky knows that if parents want to switch, there is not much the instructor can do except to be gracious about the situation. That's all right by her, Becky lies. "I wish you and Vicky all the best," she says. When switching coaches, it is important to make sure all the bills of the first instructor are paid. John being a member of PSA has the obligation to call Becky and find out if there is any bill outstanding. John cannot start teaching Vicky until all bills are paid. This seems minor; most coaches, one would think, are paid by their clients, but it is surprising how many unpaid bills exist in skating rinks.

The Pleasant Part in the Coach Change

Anne now has to talk to John. She looks forward to that. She calls him that same morning. Vicky had said that she would love to skate with her friends at the unearthly hour of 6:00. Would she? Some things just have to be put on the Wait and See shelf. John is very friendly over the phone and suggests meeting the next morning.

John tells Anne about nutrition, off- ice conditioning, and ballet. He explains that if Vicky really wants to take skating more seriously, sacrifices on all sides of the family will have to be made. The first hurdle is obviously the early hour. However, most dedicated skating mothers or skating fathers go through the early morning routine at one time or another. In eight months 5:30 a.m. will seem quite normal.

John mentions that Vicky should join the club most of his students belong to. Once belonging to a club Vicky will start working for USFSA tests. The Pre-Preliminary Move test will be the first one. Can Vicky get up so early? Will this commitment prove too much for Vicky, for Anne herself, for the rest of the family?

FOURTEEN

What Skating Can Do for Children and Teenagers

Competitive skating is a big commitment. It means long years of training, many hours spent at the rink, and last but not least, paying a lot of money. I have already discussed the joy of skating and how good it is at keeping kids occupied in a clean and challenging activity.

To Learn Discipline

Learning discipline is a big factor. Skaters cannot doodle with homework, they often have to change clothes in the car, and must really learn to organize their time. They have to wake up early, which means going to bed early. They would like to go to a late movie but must learn to say "no" to their friends at school.

Get Over Disappointments

They must learn to get over disappointments. All right, so they are not going on to a higher competition, or they come out at the bottom of a nonqualifying event. They must learn to say to themselves: there is always next time or next year. If they really love to skate, the pleasure of doing it will outweigh the disappointment very soon.

Learn Sportsmanship

Skaters should learn what is meant by being a good sport. If you feel like pulling a competitor's hair, don't—even if you believe the result was not fair. Congratulate your rival who just beat you even it it's hard at the moment. Live with results you perceived as not fair. In such a subjective sport as skating this will happen from time to time. If skaters want to persevere in the sport they have to learn to deal with this. Parents, please explain this over and over again until you believe it yourselves.

Self Control

Skaters must learn to keep their frustration in check when a jump they had down pat one day, fails the next. They must learn to "keep the show going," smile even if they just fell in a mediocre performance. Rinks and coaches won't allow temper tantrums, kicking the ice, and such like. Skating can be very frustrating at times. (All skaters know this.) What a good thing it is to learn to keep ahold of yourselves.

Self Confidence

Skaters must nurture that little thought in their heads that says **"I can do it,"** and not be intimidated or pushed aside. Parents and coaches can help and encourage positive thinking. But positive thinking often is not just there, skaters have to work on it, business men have to work on it, mothers have to work on it, etc., etc.

Being Involved Keeps Skaters Out of Trouble

Being involved in something as all-encompassing as competitive skating will keep teenagers from mixing with the wrong peer groups and getting themselves into problems.

You Don't Just Skate to Win

It is by a long shot not only winning. Some winning will come for most skaters, maybe not the biggest competitions but surely some. That is of course fun, but all the other things that are learned are perhaps even more important. All these varied aspects of learning can be a great plus in later life and will help make a skater more successful no matter what his or her ultimate profession will be.

Commitment

To become a good skater the child has to learn to commit to the sport. To be able to commit to anything is invaluable learning for later life. If a child shows great commitment to something it is easier to transfer to other things later. Commitment to study in college, to raising a family, or anything else.

The Striving for Excellence

To strive for excellence, to try to be the best you can be is a great learning experience. Only the striving for excellence will produce the most excellent results. Let your skaters savor the exhilaration of competition. Don't stop them, but don't ask of them what they cannot produce. Know the golden mean in what one can expect and what is just too much.

How does a parent know what is a good thing to expect and what is too much? Watch occasional practices and see what your skaters can do. If they usually fall on a jump in practice don't expect that jump to be perfect in competition. If they don't practice hard, ask them why. Maybe they are very discouraged about something and you can help them by finding out. Maybe . . . it's just possible . . . they are a little lazy. Possibly the standards they set for themselves are too high. Most competitors tend to be overachievers. That needs to be discussed, because an overachiever can get very upset if his or her achievement goal does not materialize. Discuss goals with your skaters, and the coach. Set reasonably high goals, but not goals the skaters cannot possible master.

Just as I finished this chapter a letter from a former student of mine arrived from Honduras where she works in the Peace Corps. I include an extract of this letter because it shows that skating helps in many unexpected and seemingly unrelated ways.

achievement in the schools. I won't bore you with details, but it is a challenging job requiring personal initiative, self-motivation, and patience. I think skating helped me to gain those qualities.

Take care,

Amy Luebbe

FIGURE 20. Extract of a letter from a former student that I received as I was writing this chapter.

FIFTEEN

What the New Coach Has in Mind for Vicky

John has a fairly typical but rather demanding schedule in mind for Vicky. Lessions four mornings a week, 20 minutes each, during the 6:00 a.m. freestyle, plus one more afternoon of skating. John also schedules off-ice training and ballet lessons. Anne is wondering how she is going to handle all this. Even the driving is daunting. But then she reminds herself, take it step-by-step. Probably it will work out just fine. This season Vicky should qualify for the Pre-Juvenile Regional championships. Short-term goals are to teach Vicky the basic beautiful stroking which is much harder than it seems, and John, having watched Vicky, has noticed she needs work on this. Of course landing her Axel is another important goal, especially for Vicky. John will have more meetings on a regular basis with Anne and Vicky to discuss goals, making them both challenging and reachable.

It's a big day. The first skating lesson with John. Monday morning (or rather in the middle of the night for Anne), the shrill ring of the alarm wakes her up at 5:00 a.m. Anne hears Paul say, "If that isn't insane." Then he turns around in bed, pulling the covers tightly over him. He thinks if Anne wants to do that—more power to her; of his daughter he thinks, "The poor little tyke."

Meanwhile Anne has torn herself out of bed, "And this four times a week," she thinks. "Maybe Paul is right, it is rather crazy. My poor little Vicky. I'll have to wake her up. I wonder if it's unhealthy for her." Anne creeps along the corridor in order not to waken her son Rob. Just as she slowly opens Vicky's door, the poor little tyke, comes out of her room. Beaming, hair up in a ponytail, tights on, skating dress on. "I'm ready Mom," she says. At least the drive to the rink is easy. There are hardly any cars on the road at this hour. "Nobody else seems to be as nutty as we are," thinks Anne.

They arrive early. Wow, the rink is quiet. Not all the lights are on yet. One girl jumps rope, another runs up and down the stairs. Vicky stands motionless and looks at the beautifully shiny blue glittering ice, all empty, waiting for her. John comes out of the Pro room. "Hi Vicky, a little early, eh?"

"For me more than for her," replies Anne. "Chauffeurs don't have to skate, they can go back to the car and sleep," says John. "Is that why so few mothers are in

here," understands Anne. "They are sleeping in the parking lot." But no 10 horses could have pulled Anne into
the parking lot. She wants to watch. Vicky starts to put
on her skates. "Not so fast, not so fast," says John looking
at Vicky. "Have you warmed up?" "No," admits Vicky,
who had no idea what 'warmed up' meant. "Put your
gym shoes back on and I'll show you."

Vicky starts running up and down the stairs, jumps
rope, and jogs around the lobby. She throws her sweater
on a bench. Even if it means getting to the rink yet a little earlier, time for warming up your body and getting
your muscles ready is never wasted. This can prevent
many injuries caused by stiff, sleepy muscles. Stroking
really hard around the perimeter of the rink, do
crossover circles with lots of energy and push. Those are
all very good warm-up routines. As a rule of thumb,
your child has warmed up enough if she takes her jacket
off. If the skater still hangs around with a thick warm-up
jacket after 15 minutes of freestyle, she has not prepared
well enough to start jumping and spinning.

The wrong kind of warm-up. Kids have a tendency
to forget all about warm-up; they rush into the cold rink,
heave one leg over the barrier, and think they are doing
the right thing for their bodies. But that's not warming
up correctly. The muscles are cold, the rink is cold, and
the best this exercise can do is that no muscle is pulled
or hurt. So don't do it. Parents are not interfering or
being skating-mother-like when they remind their children to warm up in the lobby. In Vicky's case, for today

John is in charge. But tomorrow it's Anne's turn to remind Vicky to warm up. After skating it is also important to do some cool-down exercises, often involving more stretching than on warm-up. John will show Vicky how to do that too.

Anne moves slowly toward the bleachers. It's cold up there. Anne shivers and stares at the empty ice, not half as thrilled to see it as Vicky was. To her a nice comforter in a warm bed would look much more inviting. This sport surely demands its sacrifices.

The skaters come out. Vicky seems to be one of the smallest. They all stroke around pretty energetically. John puts on his gloves and glides after Vicky. He takes her hand and gently helps her with her rhythm. He explains edges and knee bends. Stroking is very important; it is the backbone of skating, an important component in the base mark (see Chapter 19, page 176, explanation of the base mark).

She Landed It

Hallo! A scream is coming from the ice. Anne looks up startled. She must have dozed off. Her head had dropped to one side and her neck feels stiff. Oh God, I hope nothing has happened to Vicky. Thoughts race through Anne's head. Another scream. Thank goodness, she sees Vicky very alive and very happy. She understands now what the kids are saying when they scream. They say

"**She landed it!**" Is it necessary to say what? Of course we all know, the Axel. Vicky landed her Axel. The skaters all stop and clap. Vicky does not do one, but six. Wow, Anne joins in with the clapping.

It is time to get off." "Come on, Vicky your Axel is great, really great, but school does start soon."

"One more," says Vicky, who jumps and falls.

Anne waves Thank You to John, Vicky grins from ear to ear, as they rush to school. Would Vicky have landed her Axel if she was still taught by Becky this afternoon? Probably not, but that's not Becky's fault. It was not John who was the wonder Pro. It was a combination of factors.

Vicky felt good and special that she was now a USFSA skater.

Her confidence rose. John said, "Hey Vick, now there's no reason you can't do it, is there?" A good coach can enhance a skater's confidence, make them feel good about themselves. Confidence is vital in figure skating.

As a mother you can also build confidence in your child. Encourage her, when she did well—when she deserves it.

So Monday was a red letter day for Vicky. Tuesday and Wednesday were just as good. When Emma meets Anne on the bleachers Tuesday afternoon and sees Anne's smiling face, Emma says: "So it finally came (meaning Vicky's Axel of course), well congratulations, it's about time isn't it? Wait until she starts the double Salchow. That's even worse." Really encouraging, Emma. But somehow Anne feels, rightly, that Emma's discouraging remarks were a compliment in disguise. Emma was not really happy about Vicky's Axel. That pleased Anne. If Emma was a little jealous, that meant Vicky was really getting better.

She Lost It

Then comes Friday. Vicky falls on her first three Axels. She looks upset. Flaps her hands about, and drags her toe pick around on the ice. Finally Vicky takes her gloves off and throws them over the barrier—tries six more jumps and falls on all of them. "What is she doing?" thinks Anne. "Why can't she do it? Why is she behaving like that?" It's lesson time. John skates up to Vicky and then they both skate to the barrier and talk. They talk and talk. Vicky does not do one step of skating in that lesson. Anne wonders why John does not make Vicky do more Axels and correct the mistakes. "Is that what I pay good money for?" Anne can't help wondering. If a skater loses a jump (as skaters call it) it can really be a hard exercise in controlling frustration. The skater must learn how to behave, must not throw a temper tantrum. Even worse, kick or scrape the ice, swear, or sulk around the rink. In most rinks such behavior is not tolerated. The kids are sent off the ice. That sounds like a simple and effective solution, but it is not as easy as all that. Skating is a very frustrating sport. It happens to all skaters that one day they can do something perfectly and the next day it's gone. Some kids control themselves better, others have real trouble in doing so. They are sent off the ice many times, cry, wipe their tears, go back on the ice when they are allowed to, and start the whole routine over again. So what does help? Patience and consistency. After a while, with consistent reprimands, even the more stubborn skaters learn the correct behavior. Although the great majority of parents are in full agreement with such discipline and grateful that someone helps them control their child, a few parents may complain that they are paying a lot of money for the ice time, and half the time the child sits out. They may even threaten to go to another more lenient rink. That risk a coach has to take if bad behavior is really to be stamped out. Cooperation with the coach in this area of training is very important. Do not automatically believe your children if they say when they come home. "My coach was so mean to me again. I did nothing and was sent off the ice and Evelyn kicked the ice all the time and she, of course, could keep on skating." Watch a few sessions before you take your child's side. Call the coach if necessary. If the coach really let Evelyn kick, then that was not right. (Then the coach needs reprimanding.)

John did a very good thing just talking to Vicky in her lesson. She would probably fall on all her Axels this Friday. Today Vicky needs (what my students called with horror) a lecture. Not sympathy from the coach, but matter-of-fact instruction on how to behave on the ice. If John is clever and stops bad behavior at its roots, this lesson is worth its weight in gold. Finally John taps Vicky encouragingly on the shoulder, and she leaves the ice.

As Anne walks to the lobby to meet Vicky she feels like saying, "What on earth happened to your Axel; why can't you do it anymore?" That is the completely natural reaction, but the Axel should be a taboo subject for the moment. I suggest something like "So you and John had a good talk." Don't approve of Vicky 's behavior; it's perfectly correct to make sure Vicky understands that you *too* did not like what you saw on the ice today. Not because of her Axel (make certain there is no misunderstanding there). It's because of her toe dragging and glove throwing that you reprimand her. All these wise words have the effect that Vicky says, "Mom, why can't I do my Axel anymore?" Tears start rolling. She's only a little girl, and now she needs a hug. You've made your point about the behavior, now take on the mother role and soothe and encourage. "You'll get it back as sure as I stand here, and certainly quicker if you don't get so mad about it," may be a good approach. Show Vicky that you believe in her. (By the way, she will of course get it back.) In an Axel, she must rotate much faster than in all the previous jumps she learned. Therefore the timing must be right. At what split second the rotation has to be stopped and the jump opened up is a very delicate matter. The timing can easily be lost when a more difficult jump is learned. It takes patience and willpower and Vicky has the latter, but most learn the former.

After a few more days of struggling, Vicky gets her Axel back. Not completely consistently, of course, but well enough for her to be satisfied with herself. Her behavior on the ice at this point is without reproach.

SIXTEEN

A Description of a USFSA Test Session

A Test Session is Announced

A big note is pinned on the club bulletin board at Vicky's rink indicating times and test level. Vicky and Anne already know about this. John had told them that Vicky was ready for her Pre-Preliminary Moves and Pre-Preliminary Free Style tests. It is necessary to sign up for a test about two to three weeks in advance. The sign-up costs for a test are usually only about six to ten dollars. By the time your skater has finished testing, however, quite a few more charges will be added like ice time, food for the judges (which students have to pay for or buy), and the time the pro spends with your skater.

The test session Vicky will participate in is set for a Tuesday morning. Vicky likes the idea because she has to take off from school that day, which makes her feel very important.

Vicky's previous experience of testing was very informal. During a crowded practice session Vicky's ISI instructor was standing by the boards, skates on, holding a pencil and a colored sheet of paper. The instructor was well known to her students; they were not nervous or afraid. When they passed they got a badge for $3 and were very proud.

What to Wear?

Make sure her skates are polished. I know I have already mentioned this for competitions, but for tests it's just as important. Have Vicky wear a dress that fits well. Her hair should be tidy. Also make sure to bring a tightly fitting jacket. By all means let Vicky keep the jacket on, even throughout the test, if the rink is cold. Freezing skaters tend to get stiff and shivery and don't perform as well. Stretch-gloves are fine for Moves if it's cold (use clean ones).

It's the Day of the Test

The whole atmosphere of a USFSA test is special.. The rink is nearly empty, and very silent. The bleachers are deserted, except for a few scattered parents staring at the unused ice surface.

"Take the ice for warm-up please," shouts the test

chairman. Who is a test chairman? It is a person more like an angel than a human being. Her duties:

1. Get all the paperwork done for students who want to test and those who have tested.
2. Figure out test times and dates and argue with rink managers for ice cost and times.
3. Try to be accommodating to coaches and parents who call at the last minute for a student who absolutely has to take a test at a completely filled session.
4. Take complaints from coaches, who dare not talk to the judges and let their wrath out on the test chairman after a failed test of their students.
5. Help inexperienced trial judges and fill out their forms.
6. See to food, pencils, clipboards, and bring the judges drinks in the middle of a session.

Now comes the big point: They do all this for free. They keep on doing it. Smiling politely month after month. Parents, please be polite to test chairmen, without whom your child could not test, and possibly volunteer for this enviable job.

Back to the testers: out skate the prospective students. Their coaches huddle at the rink entrance door. They try to get the attention of their students, and give last minute advice.

"Remember your right arm."

"Keep your head up !"

"Point that toe please."

"How about using a little knee." And so on.

Shortly after the warm-up has started the judges file out of the judges' room with warm coats, holding clipboards, rule books, and pencils. Quite an imposing sight. Vicky is impressed and tries to smile at one of the judges, just to see what would happen. The judge smiles back encouragingly. Maybe they don't bite after all, thinks Vicky as she continues her warm-up.

Anne stays in the bleachers. She so wants to go down and tell Vicky one of her skate laces is hanging out of her boot. She restrains herself. Not one minute later John notices the lace as well and tells Vicky to tuck it in.

The warm-up is over. The judges are all lined up at one side of the rink. They are smiling and talking to each other. As a coach, I always imagined that the judges were discussing some vital information. Now that I am one of them, I know judges discuss very ordinary things, maybe a skating TV show or some recent results; nothing very important. They will try, to the very best of their ability, to judge fairly and correctly. It's Vicky's turn to test. Let's watch her.

One judge in particular is interested in Vicky. (That's because for a Pre-Pre test you often only have one judge per skater.) The judge is a lady with a friendly expression. Anne sees Vicky's head nod vigorously in agreement. She obviously has understood what the judge is saying and seems very willing to do whatever she is asked. The result is that all the skaters start to stroke.

Funny, thinks Anne, Vicky skates every day, practices all sorts of difficult tricks, and for a test—nothing but stroking. Good stroking is very important, as discussed before. Skaters must get a feeling of a gliding edge, which is very difficult for some skaters. Some have natural glide, they can skate forward and get from one end of the rink to the other seemingly without any problem. Others skate as if they are trying to push around on sandpaper. It needs a lot of practice and patience by both coach and student to learn to stroke well.

Vicky and the other two skaters start the test by stroking one behind each other. Anne is getting more educated by watching. All the free legs (the leg that does not skate, i.e., is free) are extended, but Vicky's seems the straightest. All toes seem fairly pointed, but Vicky's seem the most pointed. "My goodness," thinks Anne, "am I becoming like Emma with her Monica, seeing Vicky's skating through rose-colored glasses?"

Next come the edges. Forward, all skaters do well. Backward inside is a more wobbly affair. Anne is glad that Vicky wobbles just as much as all the others, because being able to see Vicky's mistakes shows her that she is realistic and wears no rose-colored glasses after all. Now, doing the spirals, Vicky excels. First of all, she has practiced spirals for a long time—all the way since her first Alpha class. Secondly, she is naturally flexible and thirdly, the ballet helps. The last maneuver is the Waltz Eight. The Waltz Eight is really somewhat of a reminder of school figures. It is supposed to be skated like the figure **8** used to be skated in two round circles. Vicky skates the Waltz Eight enormously big, The circle looking more like a greatly oversized inkblot. Anne sees John laughing and shaking his head. Well, Vicky finished. She skates up to the judge who, tells her that she passed and is ready to take her PrePreliminary free skating test. In order to take the free skating Vicky must pass the moves test first.

This free skating test consists of a series of jumps and a spin. Vicky does a nice long spin all on one spot (that's called centering a spin). The long drills Becky had made her do in FS-3 were really helpful. Vicky passes both tests. Anne is happy, and to be honest, has not really expected anything else. Except for the much improved stroking, Vicky had learned all this in ISI already. Why did people say USFSA tests were so hard? They *are* hard but Vicky took her Pre-Pre tests. These tests are to encourage the skater, give confidence. Very few skaters fail a Pre-Pre Test. It is good to watch some of the more advanced tests to see how hard they get.

The forms from the judge (where the remarks for each move are written down) are handed out. There are lots of complimentary remarks on Vicky's form, especially about her spiral and her spin. That the back inner edges need work and were wobbly was also recorded, as well as that the Waltz Eight was very fat. Anne understands this all perfectly. All the other Pre-Pre's pass as well.

Hand Back the Test Forms

Important. You can photocopy the test forms you got, but the originals must go back to the test chairman. She in turn must send the original forms to Colorado, otherwise Vicky's test won't be recorded and she must take it again.

Watching Higher Tests

It is always a good idea to stay and watch some higher tests. Seeing what is expected next and realizing things get harder at higher levels can really help the skater. Anne and Vicky watch some novice move tests. Emma has come to watch as well as she, too, wants to profit from the opportunity to see some higher tests. Emma sits down next to Anne.

"Vicky passed her Pre-Pres," Anne says.

"Oh, everybody passes Pre-Pres," says Emma, always so complimentary.

The first novice move tester goes out to skate. Her name is Amy. She also does a lot of stroking. But it must be a more difficult kind, as she does not seem to go very fast. There is a lot of noise made with her blades. The turns look so intricate, the body really has to heave itself around the sharp turns. Other turns are done quite slowly. "They must be really hard," thinks Anne. Amy is judged by three judges. The judges look stern and are silent. After she has finished she skates up to the judges. If the judges want a reskate, i.e., see a maneuver again, they can ask for it. No reskates.

"Oh I hope Amy passes this test," says Emma, "she tried it already two times." "So it does not stay as easy," thinks Anne. Amy comes off the ice looking discouraged. She had made a mistake and had hoped for a reskate. No reskate meant most probably that Amy would fail for a third time. Soon the test chairman hands Amy the judges' papers. Amy huddles with her coach and reads the comments over and over. Anne understands something is not right, and wonders how Amy's mother feels.

Anne notices that during the ice make the judges talk to Amy and her coach. There seems to be general agreement, as everybody seems to nod in the affirmative. If a coach is present it's perfectly okay for the student to ask the judges how she could improve herself. As a mother you can also ask the judges. Judges will be polite and answer your questions but it is better to have the coach come along also. Troubles with tests and questions to judges are better left to the coach.

Another tester comes out to skate. She is doing her novice free skate. Her name is Valerie and she does not skate at Vicky's rink. Valerie starts out very nicely. Very musically. Anne thinks she will pass. The first jump seems difficult for her. She skates a long time on two feet before the jump (called telegraphing in skating language). She falls. Well she has a few other chances. She can redo the jump if a reskate is given, or she can squeeze the jump somewhere else in the program. What astonishes Anne is that Valerie does not get up right away, although it's pretty clear that she did not get hurt. A spin is next. Valerie wobbles somewhat and slowly, slowly she ekes out the required rotations. Next is the combination jump (two jumps in a row)—another fall. From then on Valerie's program goes from bad to worse. Her arms hang, her speed lags, she looks as if she wants to give up. It seems a very long program to Anne. Finally Valerie finishes and stamps off the ice. She hisses something at her coach, who does not know whether to follow her or not. "Look at that!," says Emma with disgust. "How can a big girl behave like that." Emma has not raised a teenager yet. Had she, she would know that it is harder for teens to control their temper than for younger skaters. But I agree there is no excuse for Valerie's action.

This is an example of nonsportsman-like behavior. Even though Valerie did not skate a passing program, she should still have continued trying her best until the end. Valerie probably often gets upset and in bad moods on the ice during practice. What you do in practice, you often repeat during performances.

Parents, do help skaters to control their behavior. Remember when Vicky threw a tantrum when her Axel was not working? Anne and John stopped Vicky's behavior then and there. Probably Valerie is not taught firmly enough how to keep her temper in check. That is where the general educational part of the sport comes in. Valerie has embarrassed herself, her coach, and whoever was watching. Don't let that happen. Later on Anne passes by Valerie and her parents. Valerie is crying and Anne hears her mother say to her, "Oh, why could the judges not have passed you? They knew you tried this test so many times before." That is the wrong attitude. The judges did not pass this test because the skater obviously was not ready. Her discouraged way of performing can also be taken as a deduction in the presentation mark.

Judges pass a test when they feel the skater has mastered the skills demanded, and is ready to start working on the next level. The judges would not do skaters a favor to let them pass before they are ready, as they would have no end of trouble with their next tests.

The last skater is another novice moves test. Anne can hardly believe it is the same test that Amy had skated previously. This girl has so much power and speed. Stroking comes so easily, her turns seem just lovely flowing movements, not forced heaves and contortions. Anne asks Emma, "Who is that skater? She is so good." "Oh, she has been working on this test ever so long," replies Emma. Maybe she has, but that is a good thing. Don't hurry moves tests. They are to be done right and correctly to be of value to the skater. We have seen lately, in the highest competitions, that strong edges, good footwork, and a pleasant flowing skating style is becoming more and more important. Good, well-mastered moves tests can help a tremendous amount with these skills.

SEVENTEEN

From a Judge's Perspective

Parents often ask the question: "What I really want to know is, what do judges want to see?" Judges like to see that skaters are well prepared for the test they are taking, or the competition they are partaking in. Good flow and good body position are very important as well as sureness in the maneuvers they are attempting. Skaters should not attempt jumps they know they can't do, just because some other competitors have them in the program. Show what *you* can do. If a fall happens, skaters are to get up quickly and not let the whole program go down the drain because of one mishap. Of course kicking the ice or sulking is very much frowned upon, however frustrated the skater is. Remember, in big competitions judges watch many practice sessions. So tell your skater from a young child on, "Skate and behave as if judges are watching." Be polite to other skaters on the ice. Don't show irritation just because somebody skates where you wanted to jump.

I have already talked about judging in Chapter 3 under USFSA judging. I also go into judging further in Chapter 19 on "How to Read a Result Sheet." You may want to look at these chapters. For the explanation of inconsistencies in the ordinal numbers (how each judge places the skater), look at Chapter 19.

After the 2001 World championship I was asked by many parents why Todd Eldridge, our U.S. Skater, did not come in second place. The Russian Alexei Yagudin came second, although because of his injury he made quite a few mistakes. Todd had to be content with the bronze medal although he skated a flawless program; however, not attempting the difficulty which Alexei had. This is a difficult question which really only arises in high class competition. Who is really the best skater? All mothers agreed that Alexei is the better skater. Who should have won that day? Again, nearly all the parents agreed it should have been Todd. How should judges take the phrase "Let the best skater win?" Does it mean the best skater that particular day, or does it mean the best skater who just this one competition out of very many this year had a rough day due to injury. Think about it . . . . maybe there are two right answers to this question?

EIGHTEEN

Vicky is a Juvenile at Regionals

Vicky is now 10 years old. She has successfully passed all her tests to qualify for Regionals at the Juvenile level. Last year she entered Pre-Juveniles. It was fun but really not that much different from other nonqualifying competitions. This year Vicky is a Juvenile skater who, if she does extremely well, has a chance to go on to Junior Nationals. John had said it was very hard indeed to make it out to Junior Nationals because over 100 juvenile skaters were in Vicky's Regional event. He said that to make it to the final round should be Vicky's goal. That is a sensible goal for a lot of skaters. Parents should trust the opinion of the coach. Most coaches can assess the ability of the student realistically.

What parents tend to do is to figure out what other

skaters will likely be in the group in which their child is to skate. They spend hours looking up last year's programs or recent nonqualifying result sheets in order to predict who their child is likely to beat or which would be a hard group. That is not only a waste of time, it is also bad for the skater to hear, for example, "Of course if you pick a group with Madeline in it you can't possibly win." First of all, every skater first has to skate. Unforeseen things can happen at every competition. Secondly, it makes a skater feel afraid and already in a losing frame of mind if the group sheet comes out and the dreaded Madeline is in the same group. Many parents keep comparing their skaters with skaters from the rink at which they skate. They often forget there are many rinks, and who knows how all these other skaters perform? In Vicky's case, John had said "final round" and that should be enough for Anne. If Vicky dreams of a possible spot at Junior Nationals let her, but as a mother be realistic and be there to comfort your child if the dreams don't quite come true.

Some parents think that last minute practices are so important they sign their children up for too many. The more advanced the skaters gets, the better they know that excessive practicing right before competition does more harm than good. If a jump works well, why do 20 of them? one or two out of the 20 won't work and the skaters may become overly worried about the few jumps they missed.

What about Swimming in the Motel Pool?

Most motels have swimming pools, and most kids love to hop into them. There used to be a theory that swimming made your muscles loose and was very bad for skating. Off-ice trainers I have talked to did not share that view. However, why not wait with the pool until after competition? Swimming does tire the body out.

Goal Setting for the Performance

Ready to skate Vick?" says John as Vicky comes to the rink. John talks to her about her performance. Anne quietly gets out of the way, as she rightly feels this is a private conversation between coach and student.

"You know competition is not about beating people. It's about achieving the goals you set for yourself. Now what do you want to do at this competition?"

Vicky replies promptly, "I want to skate a perfect program with no mistakes."

"Is that not a bit much? All skaters want to do that all the time, but it does not always work. If it does it's great, but let's be a bit more specific. Is there anything special you would like to achieve in your program?"

"I want to land my double Lutz double toe, and my other combinations."

"I agree Vicky, to land the combinations in your program should be your goal for today."

Vicky feels very comfortable now. To land her combinations was much less worrying than to do a completely perfect program. She still wants to show everybody what a good skater she is but the pressure is now much less. As parents you can also help in setting achievable goals for your children. It's not that easy because you don't want to expect too much or too little. Too much makes skaters nervous because they fear they can't reach such a goal; too little does not calm the skaters down, but just makes them feel you don't think very much of them.

It is always a good idea to discuss goal setting with your coach. Skaters who know they have a chance to make it to Nationals should not shy away from telling the coach about that goal. Parents should keep their ambitious goals quiet. Let the coach make the goal setting decisions. For Michelle Kwan it was a realistic goal to expect to win Worlds. But we never heard her talk about it; what she kept on repeating was that she felt good and hoped to skate her best.

What to Do Before Going Out to Compete is an Individual Matter

Vicky, temporarily left by John wonders what to do next. If dress and skates are in order, it is good to let the skater run around a bit. Talk to other competitors, look at the vendors' stands (Vicky would like every skating dress the vendors are selling). Or she may watch another group from the bleachers. Closer to competition the skater needs to concentrate, and find the coach. Of course if the skater wants to be in private that is completely her choice. Younger skaters tend to be more social, as older ones often prefer to be alone. I had a skater who sat rolled up in a pink blanket, huddling by her mother in a corner on the bleachers. They both looked as if they were going to be tortured. Obviously don't do that. Let the skater have fun as long as it does not distract from concentration.

Starting Orders

Starting orders were already discussed (Chapter 4). Who magically arranges starting orders? As it says in the *Rulebook*, starting orders "shall be drawn by the Chief Referee or chair of the competition in the presence of at least two judges or other officials at any convenient time after the closing entries." (2002 *Rulebook* p. 47). So there is no evil being who in some incomprehensible way makes someone skate first . . . it is just the luck of the draw. To skate first is not to be taken as a disadvantage.

Vicky's Group Is on Next

The warm-up is announced. There they go, the first six in a group of eighteen. The judges are ready, sitting in a specially marked area at the side of the rink. Dad is quite impressed.

Anne and Paul sit together on the bleachers. "I am really surprised she does not look scared," he says. Crash—Vicky goes down on her first double loop. "How bad is that?" asks Paul. What will the judges think? It's not bad. Judges do not judge the warm-up. They watch to get an impression. (At higher competitions judges watch practices with the same intention). To form an impression is not judging.

The first girl to skate stands already at the boards resting. The others get off. Anne starts to fret. Does Vicky have a Kleenex, are her skates tight enough, will John remember to make her take off her jacket? Did I rewind the tape? And on and on and on. . . . The first skater has already finished. "Was that ever fast," thinks Anne. Out comes Vicky, her jacket has come off. Vicky smiles and takes her position. Anne would like to hide inside Paul's jacket, go home, be somewhere else, or just vanish from the planet for a little while.

Of course by now Anne knows Vicky's program inside out. She is very surprised that her jumps definitely seem higher, her hands and expression also seem better, than on a usual practice session. Watching suddenly becomes easy, actually a joy. Ahh here is the longish back outside edge leading into the double Lutz-double toe. Anne is not scared anymore, and Vicky lands it very well. What Vicky has done with this performance is that she has been able to transfer her confidence on to the audience. That sometimes happens, and parents and coaches are very happy when it does. There is the final spin and the curtsey. The audience claps. Vicky gets an embrace from John, and now is ready to be talked to by her dad who, quite unlike him, runs down the bleachers to congratulate his daughter. He must have liked what he saw, thought Anne happily. "I'm proud of you" says Dad and taps Vicky on the shoulder. "Let's watch the rest of the group."

The Results Come Out

Everybody is scrambling to the wall. The kids can't wait. They push and squeeze and tiptoe to see. Some sad looking ones leave the huddle with tears welling up.

Vicky rushes from the result sheet wall holding up two fingers. She came second. She is delighted, Paul is so proud of his little girl, and Anne is pleased. Only pleased. She thinks Vicky could, or even should have come in first.

Whatever parents think of the result, keep the thoughts to yourself. Do not say, "I had you first" or, "Next time go for the gold." If you want Vicky to learn good sportsmanship you have to start by giving a good example. A good motto is accept your call, be happy for today.

Enjoy the moment. If your skater made the final round be happy and proud, don't immediately start worrying about what will happen in the final round. It will come around soon enough.

Often the skaters are given one day of rest and practice before the final round. Vicky is so happy that she can stay in the motel longer, as her final round is Saturday morning.

Her practices on Friday don't go well. She is worried. She so badly wants to come in the first four that she overtries, which results in many falls. The excitement of making the final round was so great that these practices feel like "the day after Christmas." Vicky skates as if all the spunk she had was used up in her performance. John handles it well, makes her do a lot of single jumps, parts of her program without jumps, and lots of spins. That some practices at competitions don't go well happens to many skaters. Parents do not take this too seriously. Don't reprimand your skaters, saying things like, "Now why did you not try harder on practice, why did you fall all the time?" That is what the skaters also don't know and therefore obviously can't answer, except with a sulk. When parents should reprimand is when the behavior on practice was bad. When the skaters sulked, did not get up right away after a fall, argued with their coach, etc. However badly a practice goes, as a skater don't "let on"; don't show the spectators that you are miserable and mad at everything. There may well be some judges watching, and bad behavior on the ice is one thing judges really don't like.

The parents' job is to try to get the mind off skating when the skaters come off the ice after a bad practice. Going out to eat in a fun restaurant, meeting with other parents and their skaters, seeing a sight the town offers, are all good ideas. Avoid tiring your skaters out, of course. They are at a competition, not a sightseeing tour.

The Final Round

The bleachers are more crowded. The Pros wear nicer clothes. The skaters in Vicky's group are all good skaters. There is not the odd skater who Vicky knows she can definitely beat. It's Vicky's turn to skate. The same music, the same dress, the same child and yet Vicky looks very different from the initial round. She skates much slower to make very sure she does not miss. This cautious skating changes her timing and she does miss the double Lutz. She comes off disappointed. It's John's turn to talk to her, which he does for a long time. (How to handle Vicky as parents, see Chapter 8, p. 75).

The results come out and Vicky came in sixth. After a few minutes of looking miserable she perks up again. Had she not wanted to come in fourth so badly, she may have skated better. But who knows? All in all it was a good Regionals for Vicky. She is alternate; if number four and five get sick she may still make it to Junior Nationals, although this is unlikely.

NINETEEN

How to Read a Result Sheet

Let's go back to the results of Vicky's initial round program. Her parents buy a copy at the registration desk. A USFSA result sheet seems complicated at first sight, but it is the fairest way of placing skaters, and after a while it becomes quite easy to read. See example result sheet on page 168.

Ordinals—The Majority System

The first numbered names are the names of the judges (I use imaginary names for all judges and skaters; Vicky is imaginary anyway). The numbers with a dash after them (-) correspond to the numbers of the judges (to make it easier to identify them). For example, Judge No. 1-

FIGURE 21.

EXAMPLE RESULT SHEET, MAJ, TOMs, TOs, and TIES

Regional championships
Freeskate Juvenile Ladies Group A
Initial Round—Final Standings

JUDGES:
1 Hanna   2 Christiana   3 Geraldine   4 Gustav   5 Walter

	1-	2-	3-	4-	5-	Maj.
SKATERS						
1. Wanda	2	1	1	2	1	3/1
2. Vicky	1	2	2	1	2	5/2
3. Katie	3	4	3	4	6	4/4
4. Shawna	4	6	4	3	5	3 4
5. Jill	6	3	6	5	3	3/5
6. Martha	7	7	5	6	4	3/6
7. Veronica	4	5	8	9	11	3/8
	TOM 17					
8. Charlotte	8	9	9	8	7	3/8
	TO 41					
9. Barbara	9	8	7	11	8	3/8
	TO 43					
10. Geraldine	13	11	10	13	10	3/11
	TOM 31					
11. Kathleen	11	10	11	12	12	3/11
	TOM 32					
12. Hanna	⏐0	12	12	7	14	4/12
13. Susy	12	13	15	10	9	3/12
14. Lauren	14	15	13	14	15	3/14
	TIE					
15. Elizabeth	15	14	14	15	13	3/14
	TIE					

Referee   Accountant

Hanna had the first skater in second place and gave the win to Vicky. Judge No. 5- Walter had the first skater in first place and gave second place to Vicky, etc. The numbers after the skaters (without a dash) are where each judge placed each skater. These are called **Ordinals**.

Each skater receives one ordinal number per judge. The judges award two marks to each skater, one for technical requirements and one for presentation. These are displayed on a "marks verification sheet," which is taped under the result sheet at qualifying competitions only. On this sheet you can see the exact mark each judge has awarded to each skater. For example:

> Judge # 1 Hanna gave skater # 2 (in this case Vicky)
> technical mark 3.4
> presentation mark 3.6
> TOTAL 7.0

That was the highest mark Hanna awarded in the group and therefore she had Vicky in first place with an ordinal number 1.

The highest numbers on the "mark verification sheet" will result in the lowest ordinal numbers on the result sheet.

The Majority System

In the United States the results are computed on the **majority system.** This means that out of five judges the ordinals of at least three judges must agree with a specific placement (or 3 out of 2 judges, 4 out of 7 judges, or 5 out of 9 judges). In the example sheet the first skater, Wanda, has three first places. So that is easy. She is definitely number one (no one else has more first places). But it does not stay as simple. Skater number two, Vicky, has Maj.—5/2—; that means she has 5 second places. Why? The result sheet says 1 2 2 1 2— would that not mean three 2s? No, in the majority rule once the number 1 place has been given away, all the 1s become 2s (or the next lowest number). So that's why Vicky has five 2s (all her 1s have become 2s.) Let's look at some other skaters:

3. Katie, with   3 4 3 4 6 and
4. Shawna, with   4 6 4 3 5 and
5. Jill, with   6 3 6 5 3

Katie has no majority of number 3s. So all her 3s become 4s. And she ends up with 4/4s (four fourth places).As these are the lowest ordinals after the first two skaters, she is in third place. This is called a subsequent majority.

Shawna has three 4s (the 3 has already become a 4). Katie had four 4s, so Katie wins over Shawna. Katie has the greater majority.

The fourth places have been given away, therefore Jill goes to 5s (all her numbers above 5 become 5s). Jill ends up with three fifth places and therefore is fifth, and so on to the last skater.

Readers will sigh with relief that they understood that, but wait it goes on . . .

Now We Get to the TOM, and TOs and Actual Ties

Back to the example result sheet.

Geradine 13 11 10 13 10—3/11 (TOM 31)
Kathleen 11 10 11 12 12—3/11 (TOM 32)

Geraldine and Kathleen have both three 11th places. The first way to break the tie is by TOM (Total Ordinals of Majority) The ordinals making up the majority (but before they have been converted to higher numbers) are added up.

Geraldine therefore has 11 + 10 + 10 which = 31
Kathleen has   11 + 11 + 10 which = 32.

The lower ordinal total is awarded the higher placement, so Geraldine wins over Kathleen.

So far so good. But it can happen that all the ordinals of majority numbers add up to the same total. Then, we get to another tie breaker called TO. TO means all the ordinals are added (Total Ordinals).

Charlotte 8 9 0 8 7   3/8 and
Barbara 9 8 7 11 8   3/8

TOM was the same between these girls, 23 for each. That's why accounting had to go to TO. All the ordinals are added up. This gives Charlotte 41 and Barbara 43, so Charlotte receives a higher placement than Barbara.

That still is not all. If after TO there still is a tie, it stays a tie. The two last places in this event are just tied. These skaters are both happy because nobody really came in last.

To come last bothers most skaters. **It really should not matter. What matters is how skaters perform.** If they are in last place with, for them, their best performance, that is what should matter. That is really hard to understand for parents and skaters alike. If I said this already, it doesn't matter. It is important enough to say twice.

No Judges Hate Skaters

By looking at the result sheet one can find out which judge placed which skater in what place. That does not mean that one judge "likes" a particular skater better. It simply means that on this day with this performance that judge found this skater superior to the other. That is all! As a coach I often heard, "Oh that judge hates me—she gave me 11th place." That is just not true. That judge found fault with something the skater did that day. No judge HATES skaters!

(Would anybody be so crazy as to sit in a cold rink

for hours with no pay, for people [even one single one] if they hated those people—think about it.)

"Why do judges vary so much?" wonder all parents when they first see a result sheet. For example, Veronica, the 7th skater has a 4th and an 11th place. Skating is not a measurable sport like running, where the stopwatch is the judge. It is a subjective sport and all skaters and parents have to become reconciled to the fact that sometimes they won't agree, or like the result. There is some consolation—out of five judges there often is one ordinal the skater likes. (Veronica liked her 4th place) If one judge differs, the others even out the differences. Veronica did not come in 11th or 4th, but 7th, a very fair result. Another reason is that not all judges put the emphasis on the same things. One judge likes speed very much, the other really has his eye on how the jumps are done, and the third puts a lot of emphasis on good spins. I mentioned before, *no judge hates skaters*. If one skater really has weak spins and lovely jumps, the one judge who looks very carefully at spins may have this skater in a lower place every time he judges her. The skater and her parents say to the coach:

"See, I had Mr. X again, and he again put me so low. He hates me." No, he does not hate the skater, he just did not think the spins were good. (My advice: improve your spins.)

Looking at a result sheet, there will nearly always be a division into three groups. The best group will have mostly low ordinals; the middle group will have "middleish" ones, the weakest group will have the highest ordinals. It has always amazed me as a coach that even if the individual lines of a result sheet can look very up and down, the overall placements come out right. Now, being a judge, it still amazes me. Judges, I found when I started to trial judge, *really are very knowledgeable.* As coaches and parents one is quick to criticize. As a judge one learns how hard it is, how each of the judges try to get it "right." How they agonize over a mistake (and mistakes do occur, judges are also only human).

The Median Mark

After the first competitor skated there is an announcement: "There will be a small pause while the median mark is figured out." Parents wonder what is happening. They can't quite hear the muffled announcement and think, "Now what's wrong?" Relax, nothing is wrong. I am quoting from the *Rulebook* 2001,

> *"Immediately after the first competitor or couple in any event has skated, the Referee shall privately ask individual judges for their mark(s), before any deductions or penalties, and shall then inform all judges of the median mark. The judges may, at their option, change their mark(s)." (USFSA 2001 Rulebook, CR 15.03c, p.51)*

Why a median mark? Because this will present a more uniform display of marks, even though it will not change anything in the final results. When open judging is used (that's when the judges hold up their marks as one sees on TV), there will not be wide discrepancies between each judge (that is, if the judges choose to use the median mark). If there were no median mark, one judge starting really low would not be appreciated by the audience. (For example, he gives a 3.9 when most other marks are in the high 4s for the first competitor.) The spectators would "boo" the poor judge each time he holds his marks up, even though he has to stay low for all the following skaters, to be fair to the first skater. Remember the total marks are only important for the one judge's relative placement. For example, let's imagine on the result sheet (p. 168) the first judge, Hanna, has not taken the median mark and gives 1.8 and 1.9 to Wanda (Hanna's best marks given) and 1.8, 1.5 to Vicky (Hanna's second best marks given). Hanna will have Wanda in first and Vicky in second place. The third judge, Geraldine, has also not taken the median mark and gives 5.9 and 5.7 to Wanda (Geraldine's best marks given) and 5.2, 5.5 to Vicky (Geraldine's second best marks given), even if the added numbers are quite different. The results come out the same. Hanna has Wanda in first and Geraldine has Wanda in first place also. Had these judges chosen to take the median mark, this discrepancy in the marks would not have happened. (I exaggerated the enormous range just to make the example clear.)

The Mystery of the Base Mark

A base mark is the mark given to each skater by each judge on the overall quality of the competitor's skating. (That is where as mentioned before good stroking comes in.) The flow, the musicality, the speed into and out of jumps, etc. It is the mark given before any deduction or extra points are taken into account. How high or low it is only matters in comparison with base marks given to the other skaters *by that judge.*

A disappointed mother asks an official. " My Johnny did a double Lutz and Max did a single Lutz and yet my Johnny was beaten by Max."

"Yes, but look at the base mark. It must have been so much higher for Max," says the official. "Why?" the bewildered mother wonders. "And how am I to "look" at a base mark, whatever that is?" She politely agrees. Really she has no idea, but feels too embarrassed with her own lack of knowledge to ask further. (She should have—officials are always ready to help.)

What happened with these Lutz jumps? Johnny's double Lutz was very small and scraped, and some rotation was missing as well. True, he did not fall and he landed on one foot, but he practically came to a standstill. Max's single Lutz was very fast and very high with wonderful speed coming out of the jump. Pleasing to watch and a good basis for a double later on. Granted the double Lutz is harder, but in this case the basic skating, the flow and the speed of Max's jump added more to the mark than the rather "skimpy" attempt of a double by Johnny. Therefore Max got the higher base mark.

In short programs there are "deduction sheets." Judges have to take off points for mistakes. In Novice Ladies, for example, a skater is asked to do an Axel or a double Axel, the double Axel being much harder. The first skater does a nice Axel for which she gets no deduction because she has a choice of a double or single. The next skater does a very fast, completely fearless, very high double Axel, but right at the end slips off her edge and falls. She has to get a deduction for a fallen jump, actually the full 0.4 points. As the results come out, the fallen double Axel has beaten the nice single Axel. Why? Because most judges felt the attempt of the double Axel was, even with the fall, outstanding. They took 0.4 off as a deduction, but increased their base mark because it was done so very well. Good luck to the Pro who has to explain that to the single Axel skater and parent.

Ranges and What Must Be Considered in the Technical and Presentation Marks

Marks are usually given according to the group the skater is in; in a beginning group marks are in the 2.0 to 3.0 range. As the groups get more advanced the marks respectively go up. For Seniors the marks can be 4.5 to 5.0 and for Worlds they are often 5.8, and the occasional, but still very rare 6.0.

"In the marking of *Technical Merit,* the following must be considered:

    a. Difficulty of performance (with no credit being given for portions thereof which are missed);

    b. Variety;

    c. Cleanness and sureness;

    d. Speed."(2001 Rulebook, *SSR. 4.12, p.123)*

4

"In the marking for *Presentation* the following must be considered:

    a. Harmonious composition of the program as a whole and its conformity with the music chosen;

    b. Variation of speed;

    c. Utilization of the ice surface and space;

    d. Easy movement and sureness in time to the music;

    e. Carriage and Style;

    f. Originality;

    g. Expression of the character of the music." (2001 Rulebook, SSR. 4.13, p.123)

In free skating the presentation mark is the tiebreaker, should a judge's marks for two competitors come to the same total. In short program it is reversed; the required elements mark is the tiebreaker.

Marks Can't Be Changed

Sometimes placements can fall short of expectations. A fifth place can be disappointing for coaches, parents, and skaters. The top four competitors advance to a higher competition, and the fifth has to stay home. One can't help thinking, "If only that one judge had given me one place higher." But then, that is competition, "The thrill of victory and the agony of defeat."

I have often heard as a coach, "She is so disappointed with doing badly again, she wants to quit." (Wouldn't that be dreadful, is implied by the parent.) What am I to say to this intended threat?

"Oh how terrible, I will go to the judges at once and see if they can change the result." Of course that can't be done and we all know that. *Final results cannot be changed.* What I do say is,

"If Alice feels so much like quitting, you know what? Let her." Don't pander to threats. If the skater actually wants to stop skating out of reasons other than having been disappointed at the odd competition or test, that is perfectly understandable and should be discussed openly with the child.

TWENTY

Sports Injuries and Weight Problems

Injuries

The first thing I would like to stress about injuries is that I am not a doctor. The coach is not a doctor and most parents are not doctors either.

A doctor who has understanding and training in how to treat sports related injuries is a very important part of a good skating team. Good doctors trained in sports medicine, like parents, coaches, choreographers, ballet masters, music cutters, etc., all help the skaters to excel.

Sports injuries *do* happen. I don't think I have known a serious competitor who never had any injuries. The question of when to rest, when to go carefully, and when to skate through an injury are often very hard decisions. If skaters break a leg two days before Nationals the decision is easy. They just can't go. However, if the ankle is slightly sprained, should they go and see how it is? Possibly rest during the practice sessions? I have seen skaters skate through injuries and do all right, but these were few and far between. If an ankle is sprained, it hurts to skate. If something hurts badly enough, the skaters cannot concentrate on the maneuvers properly and skate badly. They then get a double whammy. They hurt and feel miserable, they skate badly, and feel even more miserable. Yes, yes, I heard only too often, "It may be the only chance they ever have to skate at Nationals." But does a bad skate really help the reputation or the healing of the injury? As a general rule I would say, if the doctor says the ankle—the back—the tendon or whatever it is, is badly injured, don't compete. My experiences with injured skaters forcing a skate were nearly always bad.

However, some skaters get fearful of injuries and before a big competition very often something starts to hurt them. They think, "What if I can't skate as well as I want to because of some pain." Again, ask a doctor (even if the pain may be more psychological than real). It is much better to be safe than sorry. If the doctor thinks it's all right to skate then, yes, skate and deal with the pain. Most often the pain (if it's a minor injury) is not even felt during the performance because the skater is so concentrated on the program to be skated.

Weight Problems

How should parents handle them? At first sight these problems seem easy to solve. If the skaters are too thin, make them eat more; if they are too heavy, cut down on the food you serve them. If only it were so easy. Many parents and coaches have struggled with a child who has stopped growing and now the thighs get heavy, the program is hard to get through, and behind the skater's back everybody whispers, "Look at Kirsten, wow, has she got heavy." In our time we all know the dangerous diseases called anorexia and bulimia. Parents and coaches need to be very careful that out of a slightly heavy child a very sick anorexic child does not develop. That does not mean that every slightly heavy teenager will develop anorexia if she is told to hold off on the French fries. But weight problems are difficult. A psychologist specializing in weight problems should be consulted if an eating disorder becomes apparent. The best way to prevent such things is to eat correctly from a young age at home. The whole family, the mother, the father, the siblings. Teach your children about healthy food. Educate yourselves as parents what is healthy for an athlete and for the whole family. Read some books. I suggested some good ones earlier, but there are many others.

TWENTY-ONE

Education and Going
Away to Skate

Education

I am a firm believer that education should not suffer through skating. It is fine to be excused from gym classes, to take a summer school course in order to have more time for skating in the fall, or to take some subject by individual instruction. But as a general rule, have your skaters go to school. If some families are for home schooling out of other reasons than skating, that is of course their choice. If a child only skates, all eggs are put in one basket. If that basket falls. . . . Give your skaters other options, other things to think and worry about. Maybe the double Axel was really bad today but she got an A in mathematics. That is a good feeling, and actually helps the double Axel go on the mend. To meet other kids with other interests is a good thing too. The skating world is somewhat one-sided. To get into unsuitable peer groups at school is unlikely for skaters because they just don't have time.

Going Away to Skate. Some Skaters Opt to Go to Training Centers

What's a Training Center?

It is quite hard to give a dictionary definition of a training centers because they vary so much. I think to be considered a training center there must be dorms available so that young students can stay without parents and be supervised by dorm mothers. Or there must be families who take skaters in as paying guests. There must be coaches who have skaters going to National and International Competitions. These skaters must train there for the younger skaters to see and emulate. There must be facilities for other out-of-town coaches to take their students there for a while. There must be "in-house" choreographers and ballet masters and strength and conditioning trainers. Some training centers have a great reputation for a while and all the best skaters seem to be attracted to them, and then somehow they lose popularity and other training centers spring up.

For the Summer Only

Vicky, now 13 years old, will be competing in Novice Ladies this season.

Anne reads skating magazines, where many training centers in other towns advertise. A list of coaches including world class Pros are shown. It all sounds very wonderful. Ballet from Russian ballet coaches. Choreographers who did programs for Olympic champions. Office training from trainers of the Olympic Training Center. Weekly exhibitions. The opportunity to watch world-class competitors practice. Supervised dormitories. Anne wonders, "Should Vicky go somewhere else over the summer?" Just the summer, not for the whole year, as Anne and Paul feel strongly that the family should not be disrupted. But six weeks over the summer? She would get more independent and have the chance to skate with different skaters and make new friends.

The Pros and Cons

Even though going away sounds very attractive, think very carefully before making the move. Some training centers are definitely so crowded over the summer that skating becomes very difficult for lower test levels. (In this case I consider Novice a lower test level).

If your skater is generally unhappy with the coaching situation at the home rink, then maybe a coaching change at home would be in order. Going away for a little while does not change the situation on return.

Remember that however world renowned the coach at summer school is, if he does not have the time for skaters who will only stay a short time, his expertise does not help much. Your skater needs a solid double Axel more than a world coach. Often skaters are assigned a coach and get only the occasional lesson from the world Pro. The assigned coach is surely knowledgeable if the summer school is good, but not better than a Pro like Vicky's coach John. It matters much more to the coach at home what skaters learn and how they practice. The home coach will show the skaters off at the upcoming championships. He badly wants a skater with a solid double Axel. How the skater does makes a lot of difference to his reputation. Coaches who work with skaters for a short time return the skaters with or without a double Axel. Their reputation does not depend on whether the skaters learn the jump or not.

Financially it is definitely more expensive to go away than to stay at your home rink—travel to and from the summer school town, more expensive lessons, room and board, more expensive choreography, etc.

However, it can be a great experience for some skaters. It can open their vision in regard to skating. They hear the same things explained in somewhat different language, which may be very helpful. The greater responsibility makes them grow. Parents may be relieved not to have to drive daily to a rink in the area, which may be quite a driving chore.

Be very diplomatic when you tell your home coach that you have decided to send your skaters away to summer school. A coach never likes to lose a skater, even if it's for only a short time. If the home coach can arrange for the summer school it is often better, as he knows best which other coaches teach like he does, and he also likes to be in on the decision.

Don't have too high hopes for what a summer school can do. Some skaters love it and then it's worth it; some don't and then it's a waste of money.

To Have the Skater Move Away from Home Completely

For Whom Is Such a Move Advantageous?

There are skaters who live in areas where there just is so little competitive skating that they cannot be stimulated enough. For these competitors it is very advantageous to move away to somewhere where they can skate with good skaters they can learn from and look up to.

Then there are parents whose kids have had disappointing results, or have had exceptionally good results. These parents often think of sending their children to train somewhere else—to a new atmosphere.

Skaters with Disappointing Results:
Parents of struggling skaters often think, "Our children love to skate—we would like for them to succeed in the sport, but up to now we have not seen good results. If

we send them away, give them the best opportunity possible and the results don't get better, we know they should go into something else." Now, that sounds reasonable enough, except that in my experience it is just the skaters who have difficulties who often stay in the sport for life. They will not hear about going into something else. These skaters often become empathetic and understanding instructors, or try another branch of the sport. They only should be sent to a training center if it is no financial burden and their education does not suffer in any way.

Skaters Who Did Exceptionally Well:
Let's say they won Novice Nationals. The parents really think they have a chance to make it all the way to the top. Winning Novice Nationals will qualify them for some financial aide, so the training becomes more affordable. Are their coaches and choreographers at home good enough? Are the skaters in the home rink challenging enough? Do they get enough off-ice workout? etc., etc. These are very important questions, and often there is more than one answer. From the first lesson as a little boy, all the way to the Olympic Gold, Brian Boitano always had the same coach.

Other skaters have gone to big training centers and have also done very well. This is a very individual decision; what is best for one may not be good for the other.

A world coach will know his way around at international competitions, he will know the judges. A world coach has other skaters who are in the top echelon, he will have had more experience with the pressure these skaters feel, and will be more versed in the psychology of a champion skater. To be with other first-rate skaters on a session is an advantage. A less experienced coach may not know the ropes as well, but they can of course learn. Coaches were not born world coaches.

To Move Part of the Family to a Training Center

There is yet another possibility parents are thinking of, and that is to move part of the family to a well-known training center—often a difficult and rather disruptive decision. In many cases the father has a good job at home and cannot move with the mother and child. If it is an only child the situation is not that drastic, as no other children with different interests are involved. Olympic champion Tara Lipinsky made a compromise. She had a very good coach in her home rink, but the parents felt she needed more challenge at a rink with very good skaters. So Tara's mother took her to another rink for a lot of the year. They stayed on very good terms with her home coach, who always taught her when she was at home. Tara was an unusually gifted skater and for her to go away to skate early was one of these exceptions mentioned before. But I have seen the sad side of such moves as well. Parents get divorced because they are away from each other nearly all the time, and/or other siblings mind being pulled out of their environment if they go along; the skater for whom all these sacrifices were made does not hold up to promise and a broken family is the result.

To Move the Whole Family to a Training Center

Now this is the most drastic move of all. The husband has to find a new and equally well-paying job, which is not always easy in a training center town. Siblings have to be taken out of their schools and separated from their friends. Who knows if that whole upheaval is worth it? Where the skater will get to, and how much the move will have helped is far from certain. For example, the skater's body may change in puberty and become unsuitable for great improvements. A girl may not have the bodily strength to execute the more difficult triple jumps. A boy may grow too tall to handle triples and quads. There may be injuries and all sorts of other things getting in the way. I advise: think extra hard before you uproot the whole family for the skater.

TWENTY-TWO

When the Time to Stop Competing Has Come

In most skating careers there comes a time when skaters think of stopping skating competitively. It's a hard time. Many tissues are used to wipe away tears of indecision and frustration. From a young child, a competitive skater and their parents have always lived, dreamed, and breathed skating. They have become emotionally attached. Skaters got up early, mothers drove and drove, and now suddenly it is supposed to be all over? It is sometimes easier for the skaters to understand that improvement just does not want to come; it's harder to see this as a parent. Parents argue, "So what the double Axel is hard?" They remember how the skaters struggled with their single Axels. Of course it would be another struggle with the double. "Is that so bad?," they argue. Yes, for skaters it can be bad. They want to improve, they want to go on, but they see many other younger skaters over-take them. They are just stuck. They have not been able to master the double Axel that is often a turning point. Like the Axel is for the younger skaters, the double Axel is for the older ones. Without a good double Axel these skaters know very well they just are not competi-tive. Now, what is the parent to do? They have spent all this money, and now the skaters just want to quit. Par-ents have heard "Never give up" in this sport, and now suddenly everything is different. It is a very difficult de-cision to make but parents, keep in mind that, as men-tioned before in this book, **skating is the skater's thing.** I have not come across many situations where the child wanted to keep skating and the parents forced the child to quit. That must be the hardest situation, and can happen through a divorce or other severe fi-nancial problems.

It is much more usual that the skater does not want to compete any longer. Forcing them will not bring much success. Finishing what they started by completing the tests is a very good and educationally very valuable thing to encourage. Let's look at the options.

Take Your Tests

It is possible for competitors to change their goals from competing to passing their tests—all the way up to the senior tests, and in as many disciplines as possible; i.e., solo, moves, dance, and pairs. (Pairs may be not suitable, but I give you all the options.) The skaters get a feeling of pride and fulfillment in this way, and it allows them to gradually move out of the competitive area. High test credentials help a lot in finding good teaching positions, apart from being a good compromise of "not giving up."

Teaching

There is often the possibility of starting to teach. Some skaters have so much fun teaching that they will go on with it part- or full-time for many years.

Ice Shows

If the skater fits what is demanded by the shows, show-skating can be a very good and special experience. Many of my students and also one of my daughters opted for this. Some stay with a show for years; others do it for just a year. The learning experiences there are enormous. The skaters must get on with others who they are constantly together with; "the show must go on," even if they don't feel like smiling or skating some days. They see the world, learn different customs, and realize what it means to live out of a suitcase for months.

Synchronized Skating

Synchronized skating can be fun. There is a real team spirit because a group effort is vital to success. There are more and more competitions in Synchronized skating, some abroad and some in the United States. It is not easy, and good Move tests are often a prerequisite, but it can be a great experience. Synchronized skating does not need as much money as singles, pairs, and dance.

Judging

There are some skaters who like to go into judging. The USFSA is very interested in new young judges. It is a wonderful way to stay in the sport and does not take so much time that college or a job could not be done as well.

ABOUT THE AUTHOR

Doris Bodmer was Swiss National ladies champion and skated on the world team for two years. She has coached in Switzerland, England, and the United States for 40 years, is Master rated by the Professional Skaters Association, and has taken some of her students to Nationals. She also has a Master's degree from the University of Chicago in Germanic Languages and Literature, and taught French and German at high schools in Illinois. Currently she judges for the United States Figure Skating Association. She has four children—two sons and two daughters. The girls were figure skaters. Her advice draws on her experience as a skater, a parent, a coach, and a judge.

FIGURE 22. The author's first days of skating at age four in Switzerland.

FIGURE 23. Many years later, as I am critiquing a student as a judge.

From her first days of skating at age four, to her experiences as a judge now, many decades later. she has had so very many wonderful experiences in the sport.

IMPORTANT ADDRESSES

The United States Figure Skating Association
20 First Street
Colorado Springs, CO 80906-3697
Phone 719-635-5200
Fax 719-635-9548
Web -age: www.usfsa.org

The Ice Skating Institute
17120 N. Dallas Parkway, Suite 140
Dallas, TX 75248-1187
e-mail: ISI@SkateISI.com
Web page: www.SkateISI.com

Professional Skaters Association International
1821 2nd Street SW
Rochester, MN 55902
Phone 507-281-5122
Fax 507-281-5491
office@skatepsa.com

Please note the following errors and omissions:

Page 43 Figure 10. Is from the World Figure Skating Hall of Fame Museum. Page 45 Figure 12. Is from the World Figure Skating Hall of Fame Museum Page 89 Figure 14. Is from the World Figure Skating Hall of Fame Museum Page 168 Figure 21. Skater number 12 in the result sheet, Hanna, got a 10th Place from judge number 1- not a 0th place.